Claimed by Vesuvius

CLAIMED
by
VESUVIUS

"Then the Lord rained on Sodom
and Gomorrah brimstone and fire
out of heaven and he overthrew
those cities and all the valley and
all the inhabitants of the cities and
what grew on the ground."

Genesis

Walter H. Marx

Middlesex School
Concord
Massachusetts

The Independent School Press

WELLESLEY HILLS
MASSACHUSETTS

There
mothball lapilli insulates
skeletons of dwellings
against the destructive
hands of time.

Tortured figures,
still preserved by their armor of ash,
express unimagined torment
as they still make their last grab for air
before Vesuvius' demons
envelope them
and keep them
for centuries, centuries, centuries.

Behind the skeletons
Vesuvius dwells,
angered master, warden of each cubicle below,
that it took into its fiery arms
and has kept for centuries,
centuries, centuries.

Peter Barrett

Permission has been granted by National Geographic Magazine to reprint
Volcanoes from the June 1902 issue.

Permission has been granted by Thomas Y. Crowell Company, Inc. to reprint
excerpts from *Herculaneum* by J. J. Deiss.

Permission has been granted by University of Texas Press to reprint two maps
from *Volcanoes* by Fred M. Bullard.

CONTENTS

PREFACE

The destruction of Pompeii, Herculaneum, and Stabiae by Vesuvius in 79 A.D. is perhaps the best-known natural disaster in known history. The entire story of the finds may not be known by all, but certain facts of the excavations have permeated most countries at all levels. Needless to say, any study of the physical aspects of the lives of the ancients is incomplete without these cities, whether one desires to find out what houses looked like in those days or to learn how they made their bread — to cite two examples from a broad spectrum of possibilities.

These cities by the velocity of their destruction are time capsules (like most finds in underwater archeology) and thus are unique amongst all the land archeological sites in the Mediterranean basin (along with the buried Minoan city on Thera in the Aegean Sea). For they give us a vast insight into their population on that August day so long ago. All the texts in stone are in place, as are the unique texts painted or scratched on the walls, the renowned graffiti. Some books of selections have appeared over the years (see bibliography), but one continually gets the impression of swift editing with cursory glances at the primary source, Volumes IV and X of the great *Corpus of Latin Inscriptions.*

Such editing is not as disgraceful as it first sounds, for the stone texts are found in section XXXIV for Pompeii and XL for Herculaneum in Volume X, itself entitled *The Inscriptions of Campania,* and later one finds hidden away and jumbled together the texts found on all the miscellaneous objects in a section entitled "Domestic Instruments." The renowned graffiti of these towns (now at the formidable number of 10,477) are found in Volume IV, called *The Wall Texts of Pompeii, Herculaneum and Stabiae,* along with the texts found on jars in sections of Volume IV, which is also titled *Texts Inscribed on Earthenware.* The wax tablets of the banker Jucundus get a separate volume as the first supplement entitled *The Wax Tab-*

lets Found at Pompeii. Yet the rubrics established by the first editor in 1871 have been adhered to in successive supplements, the latest in 1970. It is a labor of love to work through the folio pages of the *Corpus,* once the system is discerned, and the recent publication of the Herculaneum texts makes wider dissemination necessary.

It is now more than a century since the basic Volume IV appeared, and thus a reader of these towns' texts, based on the *Corpus,* would appear to be justified. In our age of relevance these mute stones do speak loudly as to human nature. I have retained the divisions of the *Corpus* but have gone on to add arbitrary subdivisions to these so as to show better the classes of surviving materials. Epigraphical jargon, though most interesting and helpful, is here omitted, but the number after each text allows the reader to pursue any text into the *Corpus,* where he will see how it is to be read on a Pompeian wall with perhaps a drawing of it. It has been most rewarding to tell others of these oft-quoted but little-studied texts, and hopefully more will, as Pompeii's disentombment nears completion and Herculaneum continues its dance with its topside neighbor Resina.

To Phrontisterion
March MCMLXX

Claimed by Vesuvius

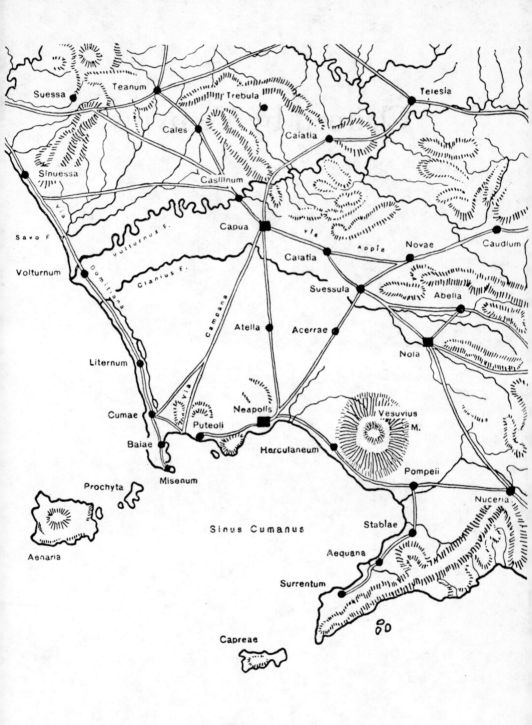

CAIUS PLINIUS CAECILIUS SECUNDUS

C. Plinius Caecilius Secundus, better known as Pliny the Younger, was born at Novum Comum in North Italy in 62 A.D. While still young he lost his father and was adopted by his uncle, Pliny the Elder. His education was cared for by his mother and a tutor. He wrote a Greek tragedy at the age of thirteen and first spoke in the Roman Forum at the age of nineteen. He was reputed to be the most learned man of his time. We gain most of our knowledge of Pliny from his *Letters* as well as from some inscriptions. There are ten books of these *Letters,* and they give us a most interesting picture of the man and the time in which he lived. We find him portrayed as a most kindly man devoted to literary studies, true to his friends, considerate of his slaves, liberal with his money. He gave a library worth $30,000 to his native town and helped a school there. Pliny held the usual offices of state, reaching the consulship in 100 A.D. It is probable that he died soon after his return to Italy about 114 A.D.

C. PLINIUS TACITO SUO S.   (*Epistulae* vi. 16)

Avunculus meus arat Miseni classique praeerat. Nonum Kal.
Septembres, horā fere septimā, mater mea ei indicat apparere
nubem inusitatā magnitudine et speciē. Ille sole usus erat, mox
aquā frigidā. Poscit soleas, ascendit locum, ex quō maxime
miraculum illud conspici poterat.   5
   Nubes ex Monte Vesuviō oriebatur, cuius forma erat similis
pinui, nam longum truncum habebat et in summō truncō ramos
latos. Nubes erat candida interdum, interdum sordida et macu-
losa prout terram vel cinerem sustulerat. Avunculus meus,
eruditissimus vir, magnum visum propius noscere volebat.   10
   Itaque iubet naviculum parari. Egrediebatur domō; accipit
epistulam Rectinae, quae erat uxor †Tasci†. Rectina imminenti
periculō perterrita erat; nam villa eius monti subiacebat nec ulla
nisi navibus fuga erat. Avunculum meum se tantō periculō
eripere volebat.   15
   Vertit ille consilium et deducit quadriremes, quod non modo
Rectinae sed multis auxilium ferre cupit. Properat ad locum
unde alii fugiunt, rectumque cursum in periculum tenet. Omnes
illius mali motus, omnes figuras oculis deprehendit, dictat, notat.
   Iam cinis calidior et densior, iam pumices etiam lapidesque   20
ambusti et fracti igni navibus incidebant. Avunculus meus paulum cunctatus est. Mox autem gubernatori, retro flectere cupi-
enti, "Fortes," inquit, "Fortuna iuvat! Pomponianum pete."
Pomponianus Stabiis erat.

GREETING: a formula where s. = salutem and *dicit* is supplied as main verb.
1. Miseni: locative case; refer to the map Non...Septembers = August 24
(see Appendix V) 3/4. ille...frigida: 'he had taken his sunbath (and) then
a cold plunge'. Later Latin frequently omits connectives. 7. pinui: for an
illustration of *this* pine see page 6. summo: 'top of'. 9. sustulerat:
from *tollo*. 11. naviculum: Pliny the Elder had his choice as admiral of
the fleet at Misenum. 15. quadriremes: heavier and not as swift as a *navicula* but with more capacity. 18. figuras: 'phases'. 23. fortes...iuvat: the
learned Pliny quotes Terence's *Phormio* (203). 24. Stabiis: the resort area
in danger.

Iam sarcinas in naves contulerat, quod periculum, quamquam   25
nondum appropinquans erat, tamen conspicuum. Eo tunc avunculus meus, secundissimō ventō portatus, amicum trepidantem
complecitur, consolatur, hortatur. Timorem amici suā securitate
lenire cupit; se in balineum deferri iubet; lautus accubat, cenat
aut hilaris aut (quod aeque magnum erat) similis hilari.   30

Interim e Vesuviō Monte pluribus in locis latissimae flammae
altaque incendia relucebant. Avunculus tamen se quieti dedit,
et quievit verissimō somnō; nam meatus animae, qui propter
amplitudinem corporis gravior et sonantior erat, ab eis, qui
limini obversabantur, audiebatur. Ille, e somnō excitatus, pro-   35
cedit et ad Pomponianum ceterosque qui vigilaverant rediit.
Inter se consultant; alii intra tecta remanere cupiunt, alii in
apertō vagari praeferunt. Nam crebris vastisque tremoribus
tecta nutabant et nunc huc nunc illuc abire aut referri vide-
bantur.

In apertō rursus lapides incidentes timebant. In apertō tamen   40
esse constituunt. Cervicalia capitibus imposita linteis ligant; id
munimentum adversus lapidos incidentes fuit. Iam dies erat
hīc, illīc nox nigrior quam omnes noctes densiorque. Placuit
egredi in litus et ex proximō mare aspicere. Ibi super abiectum
linteum recubans semel atque iterum avunculus meus frigidam   45
aquam poposcit et hausit. Deinde flammae flammarumque
praenuntius, odor sulphuris, alios in fugam vertunt, excitant
illum.

Innitens servis duobus, surrexit et statim concidit, densiore
caligine spiritū obstructō. Ubi dies redditus est. corpus inventum 50
est integrum et invulneratum. Habitus corporis dormienti quam
mortuo erat similior.

Finem ergo epistulae faciam. Tu potissima excerpe. Aliud
est enim epistulam, aliud historiam scribere. Vale!

---

25. periculum: sc. *erat* eo: 'thus'. 29. hilaris: 'a merry man'. 30. quod:
'what' 33/5 Pliny could snore well. 40. lapides: dir. obj. 42. munimentum: predicative. 44. ex proximo: 'from nearby' 53/4 aliud...aliud: 'one
thing...quite another'.

C. PLINIUS TACITO SUO S.   (*Epistulae* vi. 20)

Ego tibi de morte avunculi mei scripsi. Nunc dicis te de
casibus meis et matris meae cognoscere cupere. "Quamquam
animus meminisse horret, incipiam."

Avunculō profectō, ego reliquum tempus studiis dedi: mox
balineum, cena, somnus inquietus et brevis. Praecesserat per   5
multos dies tremor terrae; sed hīc tremor erat minus formidolosus, quod Campaniae solitus erat. Illā vero nocte tremor
increvit et omnia moveri visa sunt.

Bene mane irrumpit in cubiculum meum mater. Surrexi et
residimus in areā domūs, quae mare a tectis parvō spatiō divide- 10
bat. Hoc fecimus propter constantiam aut imprudentiam —
nescio; agebam enim duodevicesimum annum. Posco librum
Titi Livii et, quasi par otium, lego.

Ecce! amicus avunculi, qui nuper ad eum ex Hispaniā vene-
rat, appropinquavit. Ut me et matrem sedentes, me vero etiam 15
legentem videt, matris patientiam, securitatem meam corripere
conatus est. Nihilo minus ego intentus in librum manebam.

Iam hora diei erat prima, et adhuc dubius et quasi languidus
dies. Iam quassatis propinquis tectis, magnus et certus erat
ruinae metus. Tum demum excedere ex oppidō visum est.   20
Ex tectis egressi, consistimus. Ibi multos terrores patimur.
Nam vehicula, quae produci iusseramus, quamquam in planis-
simō campō erant, in contrarias partes agebantur ac, ne lapidi-
bus quidem fulta, in eōdem vestigiō quiescebant.

Praeterea mare quasi tremore terrae repelli videbamus.   25
Certe litus processerat multaque animalia maris nunc in siccis
harenis iacebant. Ab alterō latere erat nubes atra et horribilis
et vibratis discursibus rupta.

---

2. matris meae: sc. *casibus* again   quamquam...incipiam: Pliny the
Younger here quotes Vergil's Aeneid II,12/3   5. balineum sc. *erat.* 7. solitus erat: 'this is usual' Campaniae: dat. after *soleo.* 9. bene mane: 'early
in the morning'. 10. area: 'courtyard' outside the house. 12. agebam:
here 'I was in' Titi Livi: the famed Roman historian at the birth of Christ.
13. per otium: 'at leisure'. 16. matris...meam: sc. *et* as connective. 19.
dies = lux. 20. visum est: 'it seemed best'. 23. contrarias: 'opposite'.
27. ab...latere: in our idiom 'on the other side'. 28. vibratis discursibus:
'zigzag flashes of lightening'.

4

Tum vero idem ille ex Hispaniā amicus avunculi acrius matri
meae "Si frater," inquit, "tuus vivit, cupit te et filium tuum   30
esse salvos; si perit, vos esse superstites cupivit. Cur igitur
cessatis evadere?" Respondimus nos, de illius salute incertos,
nostrae saluti non consulturos esse. Non moratus ille ultra
proripit se et periculō aufertur.

Nec multō postea nubes descendere in terras, operire maria.   35
Tum mater orare, hortari, iubere me fugere: me enim posse
iuvenem, se et annis et corpore gravem fugere non posse. Ego
contra sine matre salvus esse recuso. Deinde manum eius amplexus, eam addere gradum cogo.

Iam cinis cadit, adhuc tamen rarus. Respicio, densa caligo   40
tergis imminebat. Audivimus ululatus feminarum, vagitus in-
fantum, clamores vivorum: alii vocibus requirebant parentes,
alii liberos, alii coniuges. Hi suum casum, illi casum suorum
miserabantur. Plures aeternam illam et novissimam noctem
mundo interpretabantur. Ego ipse me cum omnibus, omnia   45
mēcum perire credidi.

Tandem illa caligo quasi in fumum vel nubem discessit. Mox
dies verus, sol etiam effulsit, luridus tamen, qualis esse solet
cum deficit. Omnia erant mutata altōque cinere, tamquam
nive, obducta. Regressi sumus Misenum, et suspensam dubi-   50
amque noctem spē ac metū exegimus. Metus praevalebat;
nam tremor terrae perseverabat.

Nos tamen, quamquam et experti eramus periculum et
periculum exspectabamus, abire non cupivimus, donec de
avunculō nuntius pervenit. Haec narratio non historiā digna   55
et tibi scilicet digna ne epistulā quidem videbatur. Vale!

35. multo: adv.   descendere: historical infinitives used for indicative.
36. iuvenem: appos. 37. contra: adv. 39. addere: 'quicken'. 44. illam:
with *noctem*. 49. qualis...solet: 'such as is wont to exist.' omnia...obducta:
a universal volcanic phenomenon for outlying regions, though the affected
areas can run a gamut of possibilities; the stages of this eruption (the first
such recorded) are fully confirmed by Vesuvius' later activity in history.
50. Misenum: no prep., as this is a town. 55. nuntius: either the personal
or abstract meaning is fine here. historia...epistula: ablat. after *digna.* 56.
ne...quidem: trans. before the word it surrounds.

A NOTE ON PLINY'S PINE

The type of pine referred to by Pliny in his first letter on
Vesuvius is the familiar "Umbrella" or "Stone" Pine, scientifically known as *Pinus Pinea*. The tree can grow to a height of

80 feet and is known for its long, horizontally spreading branches
that form in older trees a broad, flat-topped head. It is a tree of
picturesque habit with a trunk usually destitute of branches for
a considerable height and with its wide-spreading parasol-like
head. It is a species of the Mediterranean Basin, its northern
limit being southern France and northern Italy, but it is cultivated in the southern parts of the British Isles and is valued for
its peculiar beauty and for its large savory nuts. It can grow in
all coastal regions of the United States except for the Northeast.

6

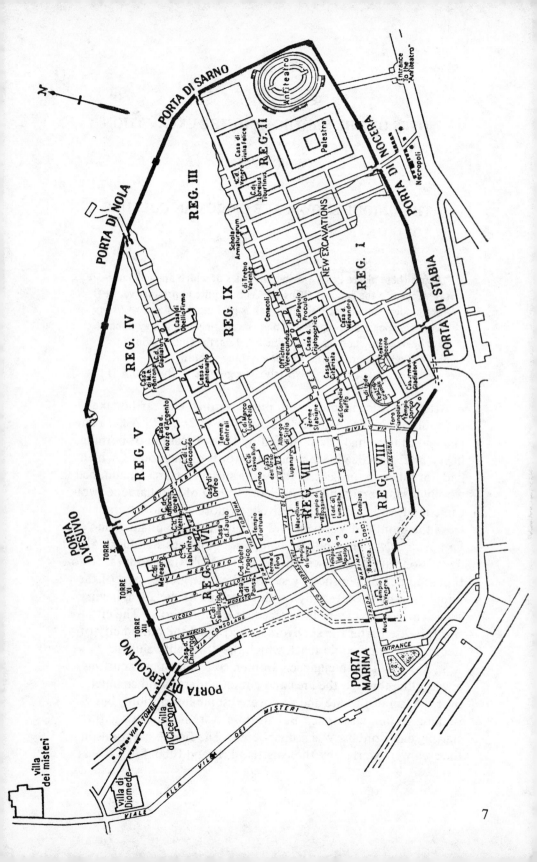

7

NOTES ON THE HISTORY AND THE EXCAVATION

OF POMPEII

THE UNIQUE SHOWPLACE OF ROMAN CULTURE

"Above these places lies Vesuvius, the sides of which are well cultivated, even to the summit. This is level but quite unproductive. It
has a cindery appearance; for the rock is porous and of a sooty
color, the appearance suggesting that the whole summit may once
have been on fire and have contained craters, the fires of which
died out when there was no longer anything to burn."

Strabo, *Geography,* V. 8   (10 A.D.)

After the volcanic dust-mud, pumice stone, and earthquake
eruption of Mt. Vesuvius on August 24th to 26th, 79 A.D., Pompeii and Stabiae had been covered by the vertical fall of burning,
heavy matter so deeply that only the roofs of the houses, which
had not fallen in, projected above the surface. Herculaneum had
wholly disappeared under a horizontal flow of rain hardened volcanic mud, which rose progressively as more and more burst
from the mouth of Vesuvius and which was more pliant than
Pompeii's ashes and lapilli so as to leave buildings standing. All
decay done at Pompeii was by moisture, NOT fire and lava. Two
thousand people perished by suffocation, the greater part of the
population having left early on the morning of the 24th, having
sufficient warning from the preceding earth tremors. The city
was forgotten after the survivors had stripped the buried city of
items which they could reach which they thought valuable.

In 1594 an Italian engineer, Domenico Fontana, was cutting
a water line through the area and cut an underground channel
over the top of the site and discovered some inscriptions, but
nothing further was done. But the hunt for antiquities was
starting and Fontana was remembered. The first excavations in
the area were started by the Austrian Prince d'Elboef in 1709 at

8

Herculaneum. Elboef's glorified treasure hunt ceased when he was unable to find any more statues for his villa. After Elboef's return to Austria his action roused the interest of King Charles III of Naples, who had the excavations continued as a treasure hunt. In 1748 Charles visited Fontana's water channel (which he thought was Stabiae) and decided that this site was more promising than Herculaneum, and so in March 1748 excavations were started at Pompeii which still go on.

Important discoveries were made at both cities, but the excavations were conducted without system and careful notation, as archeology had not yet become a science. Politics in the yet un-united Italy caused all sorts of interruptions. Finally in 1860 Giuseppe Fiorelli became the director of excavations and put an end to haphazard digging and systematized and reorganized the whole excavations with the wholehearted support of the new Kingdom of Italy. To Fiorelli Pompeii owes its greatness in this, its twilight. Fiorelli's ideas have been maintained: a journal is kept meticulously; there is care and preservation of excavated buildings and objects; and rubble is disposed of, as each part of the city is worked on, one by one. The days of treasure hunts for filling museums were over. The aim is to uncover everything but to leave the city like the Pompeii of 79 A.D. and restore everything when restoration is sure.

The amazing thing about Pompeii is the marvels done with the people, animals, and plants that were living in 79. During the excavations the archeologist comes across hollows which Fiorelli recognized as the forms of bodies preserved by the petrified ash and cinder. By pouring plaster into these hollows reproductions of the above named objects are obtained in the most precise detail at the last moment of their life. This technique, invented by Fiorelli, has enabled archeologists to determine that the athletic fields of Pompeii had been surrounded by tall plane trees before the disaster. The trees themselves have vanished completely, but the space left by their root systems has been filled with cement or plaster. Thus the nature of the roots indicated the size and the variety of the tree. Similarly for the gardens of Pompeii.

At the present time about 80% of Pompeii has been excavated

mostly under the direction in this century of Andreo Maiuri, who
waged a stalwart defense of his life's work, especially during
World War II. Objects found are to be seen in the Museum at
Naples or Pompeii or just where they were on the fateful August
day. The subsequent eruptions of Vesuvius, including a spec-
tacular one in 1944, seen by many American GI's, have managed
to leave Pompeii alone. Not so war! For in April 1943 Allied
reconnaissance patrols flying above the city thought that they
had detected a German panzer division hidden in the ruins.
(There was none.) The first bomb struck the Forum. It was
followed by 150 more bombs. Damage was enormous. The
monuments that had been reconstructed with so much toil were
once again demolished and covered and work had to be done
again, where possible. And so the research and work on one of
the world's most famous and romantic cities goes onward.

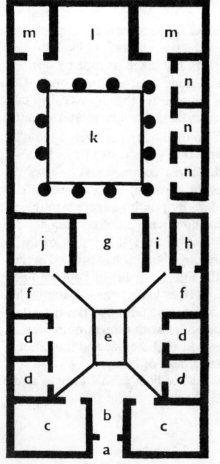

GENERAL GROUND PLAN OF
A POMPEIIAN HOUSE

a.   *vestibulum*
b.   *fauces*
c.   *cellae*
d.   *cubicula*
e.   *atrium*
f.   *alae*
g.   *tablinum*
h.   *apotheca*
i.   *andron*
j.   *triclinium*
k.   *peristyle*
l.   *exedra*
m.   *osci*
n.   *cubicula*

AN ALBUM OF POMPEIAN INSCRIPTIONS

More than 15,000 inscriptions have been found at Pompeii, covering the wide field from formal commemorative tablets to scribblings on walls, doorposts, pillars, and tombs. We are here mostly concerned with the latter, though a few examples of the former are given. The latter variety are so interesting because of their volume in this one place. They were done by all sorts of the common people: slaves, schoolboys, loungers, policemen, and lovers. These were made with a stylus (*graphium*), the pencil or ballpoint pen of the ancient world, or sometimes drawn with charcoal or chalk or even paint with a *scriptor* hired to do this (like our billboards on highways). The height on a wall tells the age of the writer most of the time. Love is the most prominent theme in prose or verse. Yet these *graffiti*, as these scratchings are technically known, are not to be disregarded, for they give a lively idea of individual tastes, passions, and experiences. There are several kinds: monumental inscriptions (engraved on stone), public notices (painted on walls), graffiti (private notices scratched on walls), and business inscriptions in their own class. In the election notices, which are usually painted on walls in a bright red paint by a *scriptor,* about 100 candidates are met.

Pompeii was founded in the 6th century B.C. by a native tribe of Oscans and was Romanized about 100 B.C. It was a popular resort town, Cicero himself having a villa there of which he speaks frequently in his *Letters.* It was a "secondrate" town but was active commercially, carrying on much business as can be seen from the shops on Abundance Street (see map). Depending on the time of year, its population varied, but a good figure would be about 35,000. It was governed by a *decurio* (city council) and had two kinds of officials: two *duumviri* for law (mayors), *aediles* for supervising the police and games (commissioner), and *quinquennales,* who were elected every fifth year for special tasks (special mayor). These held office for one year.

The extraordinary thing is not only that these inscriptions

are scrawled upon the walls of Pompeii, but also that they have been preserved to us. The inscriptions were sometimes made by people who did not have the most brilliant acquaintance with the alphabet and so are here edited into good Latin. Again, the way they appear on walls is difficult to decipher (see illustrations) and they must be transcribed into letters with which you are familiar. Thus these inscriptions allow a novelist like Sir Edward George Bulwer-Lytton to grace the pages of *The Last Days of Pompeii* with actual names which, could the original Pompeian but read it, would give him quite a shock. With these inscriptions, the found implements, and the ruins of a town buried alive, what a vivid picture may be had of life in that town of so long ago! This has been nicely done recently by Jack Linsay in his novel, *The Writing on the Wall.*

In our own culture we have graffiti, which indeed would make a most interesting commentary on our times. Similarities will be noticed as you read the inscriptions below — both in the form and in the persons mentioned. The numbers after each refer to the number in Volume IV of the *Corpus Inscriptionum Latinarum,* unless otherwise indicated. For the formal inscriptions engraved on stone occur in Volume X. The section on this latter variety is extensive so that a taste of this type of inscription, usually still in place at Pompeii, may be gained. The Wax Tablets of the businessman, Jucundus, will be studied separately (see pg. 44)

> "We are handling original documents without the intervention of copyists which stands between the author of a Greek or Roman masterpiece and the modern reader. The shapes of the letters and the spelling are just as they were left by the stonecutter or the scribbler; the various handwritings can still be as plainly distinguished on the charcoal tablets of L. Caecilius Jucundus as though the signatures were witnessed only yesterday. Through the inscriptions we are brought into contact with the personality of the Pompeians as in no other way." — A. Mau, trans. F. W. Kelsey.

THE FORMAL TEXTS OF POMPEII

from the West Side of the Forum:

M. Holconius Rufus, duovir iure dicundō tertium, (et) C. Egnatius Postumus, duovir iure dicundō iterum, ex decurionum decretō ius luminum opstruendorum HS ∞∞ redemerunt. *(787)*

from one of the statue bases in the Forum:

C. Cuspio, Cai filio, Pansae, IIviro iure dicundō quartum, quinquennali, ex decurionum decretō pecuniā publicā. *(790)*

on the Mensa Ponderaria in the Forum:

A. Clodius, Auli filius, Flaccus (et) N. Arcaeus, Numeri filius, Acellianus Caledus, duoviri iure dicundō, mensuras exaequandas ex decurionum decretō. *(793)*

on the Colonnade of the Forum:

Vibius Popidius, Epidi filius, quaestor, porticus faciundas coeravit. *(794)*

on the altar of the Temple of Apollo just off the Forum:

M. Porcius, Marci filius, L. Sextilius, Luci filius, Cn. Cornelius, Cnaei filius, A. Cornelius, Auli filius, IIIIviri, de decurionum decretō faciundum locarunt. *(800)*

L. Sepunius, Luci filius, Sandilianus (et) M. Herennius, Auli filius, Epidianus, duoviri iure dicundō, de suā pecuniā faciundum curaverunt. *(804)*

GENERAL NOTES: 1) The tripartie Roman name is usually split by a patronymic; trans. the whole name and then the patronymic. 2) Consult the vocabulary to get exact modern equivalents for the Latin titles. 3) HS is to Romans what $ is for us. 4) much language on the formal texts is formula, which will only be given once *in these notes.* 5) an ordinal numeral in the neuter means 'for the ___ th time'.
787. ex: 'according to'. HS: expressing the sum paid ∞: more commonly written as M. 793. exaequandas: sc. *hoc altare* as subj.

13

the elogia on either side to the entrance to Eumachia's Place:

Aeneas, Veneris et Anchisae filius, Troianos, qui captā Troiā bello superfuerunt, in Italiam adduxit. Bellum suscepit . . . oppidum Lavinum condidit et ibi regnavit annos trīs. In bello Laurenti subito non conparuit appellatusque est Indigens Pater et in deorum numerō relatus est. *(808)*

Romulus, Martis filius, urbem Romam condidit et regnavit annos duodequadraginta isque primus dux, duce hostium Acrone rege Caeninensium interfectō, spolia opima Iovi Feretrio consecravit receptusque in deorum numerum Quirinus appellatus est. *(809)*

above the rear entrance to Eumachia's Place:

Eumachia, Luci filia, sacerdos publica, nomine suō et M. Numestri, Frontonis fili, chalcidicum, cryptam, porticus Concordiae Augustae Pietati suā pecuniā fecit eademque dedicavit. *(810)*

near the Forum Baths:

L. Caesius, Cai filius, duumvir iuri dicendō, (et) C. Occius, Marci filius, (et) L. Niraemius, Auli filius, IIviri, de decurionum sententiā ex pecuniā publicā faciundum curarunt probaruntque. *(817)*

on the shrine's architrave in the Temple of Fortuna Augusta:

M. Tullius, Marci filius, duumvir iure dicundō tertium, quinquennalis, augur, tribunus militum a populō, aedem Fortunae Augustae solō et pecunia suā. *(820)*

on the Stabian Baths:

C. Uvlius, Cai filius, (et) P. Aninius, Cai filius, duoviri iure dicundō, laconicum et destrictarium facienda et porticus et palaestram reficienda locarunt ex decretō decurionum; ex eā pecuniā, quod eos e lege in ludos aut in monumenta consumere oportuit, faciundum coerarunt eidemque probarunt. *(829)*

---

808. bello: dat. after *supersum*. The dots represent textual damage. tris = tres 809. is primus dux consecravit: 'he was the first general to consecrate' 810. M. Numestri: sc. *nomine* after *et* before this name. 817. faciundum (esse): something like *hoc aedificium* with *faciundum* quod: 'because'. 820. solo: a noun sc. *dedicavit* as main verb 829. sc. *hoc aedificium* with *faciundum*

on the sundial by the Doric Temple in the Triangular Forum:

L. Sepunius, Luci filius, Sandilianus (et) M. Herennius, Auli filius, Epidianus, duoviri iure dicundō, scolum et horologium de suā pecuniā facienda curarunt. *(831)*

in the Large Theatre:

> Marci Holconi Rufus et Celer cryptam, tribunalia, theatrum. *(833, 834)*

M. Artorius, Marci libertus, Primus architectus. *(841)*

in the Small Theatre:

C. Quinctius, Cai filius, Valgus (et) M. Porticus, Marci filius, duoviri, decurionum decretō theatrum tectum faciendum locarunt eidemque probarunt. *(844)*

from the Temple of Isis:

> N. Popidius, Noni filius, Celsinus aedem Isidis, terrae motu collapsam a fundamentō, pecuniā suā restituit. Hunc decuriones ob liberalitatem, cum esset annorum sex, ordini suo gratis adlegerunt. *(846)*

from the Amphitheatre:

C. Quiretius, Cai filius, (et) N. Porcius, Marci filius, duoviri quinquennales coloniae honoris causā, spectacula de suā pecuniā faciunda coerarunt et colonis locum in perpetuum dederunt. *(852)*

A NOTE ON THE BOXED TEXTS: These texts (in copies) were incorporated into the exterior wall of Robinson Hall of the Harvard Graduate School of Design by the classically influenced architects, McKim, Mead, & White — surely they are unique in the world outside Italy.

833/4. Marci Holconi: plur. to save space with two people whose names were almost alike. sc. *aedificaverunt* 846. terrae mote: the harbinger of things to come from Vesuvius that struck in 63 A.D., whose effects are still visible. gratis: adv. 852. honoris causa: 'out of respect'.

one of a group from the Amphitheatre:

L. Saginius, IIvir iure dicundō, pro ludis et luminibus ex decurionum decretō cuneum. *(855)*

M. Cantrius, Marci filius, Marcellus, duumvir, pro ludis luminibusque cuneos III faciundos coeravit ex decretō decurionum. *(857)*

a bronze military diploma found in Ward VIII:

Imperator Caesar Vespasianus Augustus, pontifex maximus, tribuniciā potestate II, imperator VI, pater patriae, consul III, designatus IIII, veteranis, qui militaverunt in Classe Misenensi sub Sex. Luciliō Bassō, qui sena et vicena stipendia aut plura meruerant et sunt deducti Paestum, quorum nomina subscripta   5
sunt, ipsis liberis posterisque eorum civitatem dedit et conubium cum uxoribus, quas tunc habuissent, cum est civitas iis data, aut, sequi caelibes essent, cum iis quas postea duxissent dumtaxat singuli singulas.

Nonis Aprilibus, Caesare, Augusti filiō, Domitianō (et) Cn.   10
Pediō Cascō cos. Descriptum et recognitum ex tabulā aeneā, quae fixa est Romae in Capitoliō in podiō Arae Gentis Iuliae parte exteriore. *(867)*

near the east corner of a block:

Diogenes structor. *(868)*

FROM THE DOORWAYS

in the House of Faunus:

Have! *(872a)*

---

855. something like *fecit* is to be supplied. luminibus: 'lightning'. 867. A mate to this text was found at Herculaneum. Check the vocab. carefully for the imperial title. 3/4. classe Misenensi: had this man served under the Elder Pliny? sena et vicena: the distributive numerals rather than the ordinals. 5. Paestum: no prep. before a town. 6. civitatem: 'citizenship', the new meaning of this word one usually gets in Cicero's oration, *Pro Archaia*. 8. siqui: 'if any'. 9. duxissent: 'had married'. 12. Arae: no longer visible on the Capitoline Hill. 872a. Faunus must have aspirated all like Catullus' Arrius, (See Catullus 84).

16

in several homes:

Salve! *(873)*

in the house of Siricus:

Salve, lucrum! *(874)*

in a house in Ward VI:

Lucrum gaudium. *(875)*

one of Pompeii's most famous texts in the House of the Poet:

Cave canem! *(877)*

in the house of A. Octavius Primus:

Cedo, ceneamus! *(878)*

SELECTED GRAFFITI OF POMPEII

WALL NOTICES IN GENERAL

Habeat Venerem Pompeianam iratam qui hoc laeserit. *(538)*
Nunquam sit salvos, qui supra scripsit. *(1837)*
Qui hoc leget, nunquam postea aliud legat. *(1839)*
Admirer, paries, te non cecidisse ruinā, qui tot scriptorum
taedia sustineas. *(1904, 2461, 2487)*
Scripsit Aemilius Celer Invidiose, qui deles, aegrotes. *(3775)*
Quis hīc ulla scripserit, tabescit neque nominetur. *(7521)*
Quisquis hoc laeserit, habeat iratum Iovem. *(8360)*

875. sc. *est.* 878. cedo: a frozen word. 538. Pompeianam: Venus was the
tutelary deity of the city, as many paintings show. qui...laeserit: a subj.
clause of indefinite characteristic agreeing with an understood *is*, which is
subject of the sentence 1837. This oft-repeated poem often has been called
"Pompeii's greatest graffito" taedia: 'silly scribblings' 3775. invidiose:
'o jealous man' 7521. quis = quisquis.

17

THE ECONOMY

a. at the tavern

Hospitium C. Hygini Firmi *(3779)*

Sittius restituit Elephantum. *(806)*

Hospitium: hīc locatur triclinium cum tribus lectis et com-
modis omnibus. *(807)*

Assibus singulis hīc bibitur tibi; dipudium si dederis, meliora
bibes; quartum si dederis, vina Flaerna bibes. *(1679)*

Sei cope, probe fecisti, quod sellā commodasti. *(3502)*

Da frigidam pusillum! *(1291)*

Adde calicem Setinum! *(1292)*

Itis, foras rixatis! *(3494)*

Talia te fallant utinam mendacia, cope; tu vendes aquam
et bibes ipse merum. *(3948)*

b. shopsigns

Agilis mensor. *(5405)*

Successor textor *(8259)*

P. Cornelius Faventinus tonsor *(8741)*

Phoebus ungentarius

Cresces architectus

M. Vecilius Verecundus vestarius

c. at the jeweler's

Gemmam velim fieri horā nonā. *(1698)*

Ante diem VI Kalendas Novembres praebuit Surus Petilius
ornamenta M. Fauso Siloni honoris causā. *(2455)*

d. at the baker's

III Kalendas Maias panem feci. *(8972)*

VIII Kalendas Maias panem feci. *(8972)*

Panem feci feliciter. *(8973)*

e. at the cleaner's

III Idus Apriles tunica I *(1392)*

Kalendas XII Maias tunicam, pallium

Nonis Maiis fasciam

VIII Idus Maias tunicas II lavandas dedi. *(1393)*

Pridie Nonis Iulis tunica HS XV *(9108)*

1679. assibus: abl. of price 3502. Sei: the vocative of a man's name commodasti = commodavisti as usual, sc. *me* as dir. obj. Among some poems
attributed to Vergil is a poem entitled *Copa* 1291. frigidam: sc. *aquam*
3494. treat verbs as imps. 2455. honoris causa: 'out of respect' 1392. sc
vendita est 1393. all accusatives: after *lavandas dedi* 9108. again *vendita est.*

18

f. grocery lists

    oleum, libra; asses IV
    paleam: asses V
    faenum: asses XVI
    diaria: asses V
    furfurem: asses VI
    virtam: asses III
    oleum: asses VI   *(4000)*
    VIII Idus: caseum I
              panem VIII
              oleum III
              vinum III

Dies	Nundinae
Saturni	Pompeiis
Solis	Nuceria
Lunae	Atila
Martis	Nola
Mercuri	Cumis
Iovis	Puteolis
Veneris	Romae
	Capua *(8863)*

4000. sc. something like *peto* or *desidero* 8863. a list of market-days for various towns about our city (see map).

AVETTIVMFIRMVM
AED· O·V·F·DIGN·EST
CAPRASIA CVM·N·YMPH·ROG·

g. various memos:
Faenum allatum VIII Idus Octobres. *(1239)*
XVI Kalendas Februarias caro venit. *(1653)*
XIII Kalendas Februarias olei pondera DCCCXXXX *(4610)*
Oliva condita XVII Kalendas Novembres. *(8489)*
X Kalendas Februarias ursa peperit diē Iovis. *(8840)*
V Idus Ianuarias X, usurā deductā. *(10106)*

LITERATURE AND PROVERBS

a. from Virgil's *Aeneid:*
Arma virumque cano Troiae qui primus ab oris . . . *(2361,
3889, 4036, 4191, 4212, 4665, 4675, 4737, 4832, 4877,
5002, 5012, 5115, 8416, 8831)*   *Aeneid I.1*
Arma virumque *(10059, 10086, 10111a)* *Aeneid II.1*
Conticuēre omnes. *(2213, 8222)*
Contiquēre omnes, intentique ora tenebant. *(3889)*
Contiquēre. *(10096a)*
Rusticus es, Corydon.   *Bucolics II.56*
Fullones ululamque cano, non arma virumque. *(9131)*

b. mythology in action
Labyrinthus: hīc habitat Minotaurus. *(2331)*

c. some adages
Minimum malum fit contemnendō maximum. *(1811, 1870)*
Quid pote tam durum saxsō aut quid mollius undā?
 Dura tamen molli saxsa cavantur aquā. *(1895)*
Moram si quaeres, sparge milium et collige. *(2069)*
Mors, aurem vellens, "Vivite," aid, "venio".

1239. allatum: sc. *est* 8489. condita: sc. *est* 8820. die Iovis: Thursday
(see #8863 above) 2361 etc. This most frequent of Pompeiian graffiti is
always found at lower levels on walls, proving that they are children's
attempts at memorizing the great Roman epic of the early 1st century A.D.
and that Vergil's masterpiece became a schoolbook as soon as written
10096a. a spelling mess! 9131. Some child could not resist a parody of the
Aeneid's opening line! 2331. This graffito, like so many, is accompanied
by a picture (see later pages); the Cretan tale is found in all books of mythology 1895. pote: 'can be.' tam: 'as' saxo: 'as a rock', note the mispel-
ling.

20

THE ANCIENTS' BILLBOARD

Urna aenea periit de tabernā. Si quis rettulerit, dabuntur HS LXV. Si furem dabit, unde rem servare possimus, HS XX. *(64)*

Equam si quis aberravit cum semuncis oneratam ante diem VII Kalendas Decembres, convenito Q. Decium, Q. Deci libertum, Hilarum citra pontem Sarni fundō Mamianō. *(3864)*

Insula Arriana Polliana Gnaei Aillei Nigidi Mai: locantur ex Kalendis Iuliis primis tabernae cum pergulis suis et cenacula equestria et domus. Conductor, convenito Primum, Gnaei Allei Nigidi servum. *(138)*

In praedis Iuliae, Spuri filiae, Felicis locantur balneum venerium et nongentum tabernae, pergulae, cenacula ex Idibus Augusti primis in Idus Augusti sextas annos continuous quinque. Si quis desideravit, locatricem eō nomine convenito. *(1136)*

Thermae M. Crassi aquā marinā et balnea aquā dulci. Ianuarius libertus.

Ante diem XI Kalendas Iunias Ramius auctionem fecit. *(4495)*

D. Octacilius moritur. *(4777)*

Officiosus fugit VIII Idus Novembres, Drusō Caesare (et) M. Iuniō Silvanō cos. *(5214)* | 15 AD

64. unde= equo. rem = urnam 3864. quis = *aliquis* after *si*. convenito: the archaic future imperative = conveniat fundo Mamiano: 'on Mamus' estate', with prep. omitted 183. Arria Pollia: the concierge Gn. Alleis Nigidus Maius: owner. primis: 'next' 1136. praedis: a common variant for *práe*diis 5214. Officiosus: a slave 5386. sis...est: 'whoever you are'.

21

GREETINGS AND SALUTATIONS

a. Hello, Dolly!
   Hospes, salve! Salve, sis quisquis est! Vale! *(5386)*
   Ave, puella! *(10040)*
   Diogenes ubique! *(10050)*

b. Nice and not so nice
   Campani, victor unā cum Nucerinis, peristis! *(1293)*
   Nucerinis infelicia! *(1329)*
   Puteolanis feliciter! Omnibus Nucherinis felicia et uncum
     Pompeianis (et) Petecusanis! *(2183)*
   Priscus caelator Campanio gemmario feliciter! *(8505)*
   Pompeianis fel-feliciter! *(8516)*
   Pompeianis ubique salutem! *(9143)*
   Pompeianis feliciter! *(9144)*
   Fusce, cinaede! *(10086b)*

c. warnings
   Fures foras; frugi intro. *(4278)*
   Perarius, fur es! *(4764)*
   Fur, cave! *(6701)*
   Cacator, cave malum aut, si contempseris, habeas Iovem
     iratum! *(3716)*
   Cacator, cave malum! *(3782)*
   Cacator, sic valeas et tu hoc locum transias. *(6641)*
   Otiosis locus hīc non est. Discede, morator! *(813)*
   Stercorari, ad murum progredere! Si prensus fueris, poe-
     nam pati necesse est. Cave! *(7538)*
   Move te, fellator! *(8466)*

1293. Victor: the Campanians are considered one group 2183. uncum:
'hook', excl. acc. 8516. A studderer!
4278. frugi: a frozen adj. agreeing with an understood *viri* 6641. transias =
transeas.

VARIATIONS ON A THEME

Mus, cave malum! *(8645)*
Mus, vale! *(8802)*

MINI-LETTERS

Livia Alexandro salutem. Si vales, non multum curo. Si perieris, guadeo. *(1593)*
Virgula Tertio suo: indecens es. *(1881)*
Romulus Cerdoni salutem: scias volo me tui curam egisse. *(2413)*
Aemilius Fortunato suo fratri salutem. *(5350)*
Crescens Chryseroti salutem. Quid agit tibi dexter ocellus? *(8347)*
Secundus Primae suae ubique ipse salutem. Rogo, domine, ut me ames. *(8364)*

FARE YE WELL

Pupa, quae bella es, tibi me misit qui tuus est. Vale! *(1234)*
Victoria, vale! Et ubique es, suaviter sternutes! *(1477)*
Pyrrhus Gaio Heio, collegae suo: moleste fero quia audivi te mortuum; itaque vale! *(1852)*
Cestila, regina Pompeianorum, anima dulcis, vale! *(2413)*
Propero. Vale, mea Sura! Fac me ames! *(2414)*
Vale, Modeste, vale! Valeas, ubicumque es! *(4504)*
Vesbine cope, vale! *(6700)*

MERE MESSAGES

a. "Name-plates"
    Paris hīc fuit. *(1245)*
    Sabinus hīc. *(1305)*

1593. salutem: sc. *dicit,* as thruout in these mini-letters 2413. scias: sc. *ut* in a noun clause after *volo* 8347. quid agit: 'how is?' 1234. qui... est: sc. *vir* as antecedent and subj. of *misit.* pupa: vocative 1842. te: sc *esse* 2414. ames: sc. *ut* in noun clause after *fac* — *hic* from the adverbial *hic*

23

Hīc habitat Felicitas. *(1454)*

C. Pumidius Diplus hīc fuit ante diem V Nonas Octobres,
M. Lepido (et) G. Catulo cos. *(1842)*

Aufidius hīc fuit. Vale! *(6702)*

Aemilius Celer hīc habitat. *(3974)*

Urbanus hīc VI Idus Decembres. *(8596b)*

Pacatus hīc cum suis mansit Pompeianis. *(8660)*

Antiochus hīc mansit cum suā cithara. *(8792)*

Symphonus hīc IV Nonas Apriles. *(10054)*

Samus unius coronae, Murmillo idem eques, hīc habitat.

b. The royal we

Vici Nuceriae in aleā★DCCCLVS fide bonā. *(2119)*

M. Iuni insula sum. *(4429)*

Accepi epistulam tuam. *(5031)*

Hīc fuimus cari duo nos sine fine sodales; nomina si
quaeris, Caius et Aulus erant. *(8162)*

Hīc habitamus; felices nos dii faciant. *(8676)*

VI Kalendas Septembres mansimus Pompeiis. *(10202)*

8596b. sc *erat* 8792. cithara: the classical equivalent to the modern guitar.
coronae: gladiators who survived were awarded crowns. idem: adv. 'likewise' 2119. * = HS. fide: 'credit' 8676. dii = dei, as usual 9123. another
nice poetic graffito. cum: 'although'. Phoebe: the counterpart to the sun.
modo: adv. Venerum: 'love affairs'.

24

c. a poem
   Nihil durare potest tempore perpetuō.
   Cum bene Sol nituit, redditur oceano.
   Decrescit Phoebe, quae modo plena fuit.
   Sic Venerum feritas saepe fit aura levis.   *(9123)*

d. character assassination
   Stronnius nil scit. *(2409a)*
   Ladicula fur est. *(4776)*
   Albanus cinaedus est. *(4917)*
   Ampliatus Pedanio fur est. *(4993)*
   Crescens publicus cinaedus. *(5001)*

e. a date
   Ante diem XIIII Kalendas Novembres, C. Laelio Balbō
      (et) C. Antistiō Vetere cos. *(10018)*

f. best wishes!
   Samius Cornelius, suspendere! *(1864)*
   In cruce figaris! *(2082)*

g. some statements
   Ad quem non ceno, barbarus ille mihi est. *(1880)*
   Menander hic primus omnium comoedia scripsit. *(7350)*
   Malim ne amici fellent quam inimici irrument. *(1003)*

h. the weather for today
   Pluit. *(10088a)*

i. we wish you a . . .
   Saturnalia, io Saturnalia! *(2005a)*
   Ianuarias nobis felices multos annos! *(2059)*

j. to the traveler
   C. Sabinus Statio dicit plurimam salutem, viator. Pom-
peiis panem gustas; Nuceriae bibes. *(3903)*
   Viator, Pompeiis panem gustes, sed Nuceriae bibes. *(8903)*

1864. suspendere: the passive imperative here with middle (or reflexive)
force 1880. ad quem...ille: 'he, at whose home... 2005a. Saturnalia: The
end of the year festival for Saturn, Roman god of beginning & end, like our
Christmas 2059. Ianuarias: sc. *menses* in an exclam. acc. annos: acc. of
time.
3903. Nuceriae: locative, as often in the graffiti.

k. a glance back
   Sodoma   Gomora *(4976)*

LOVERS' MESSAGES

a. Kilroy was here!
   Staphilus hīc cum Quietā. *(4087)*
   Romula hīc cum Staphylō moratur. *(2060)*
   Felix cum Fortunā. *(2224)*
   Felix hīc locus est. *(2320)*

b. Cherchez la femme!
   Glyco cum Martiale; sole caliente sities. *(89)*
   Successus textor amat componiae ancillam, nomine Hiriden,
     quae quidem illum non curat. Sed ille rogat; illa commiscere-
     tur. Scribit rivalis. Vale! *(825)*
   Quisquis amat, valeat; pereat qui nescit amare. Bis tanto
     pereat quisquis amare vetat. *(1173, 3199, 4091)*
   P. Comicius Restitutus cum fratre hīc stetit. *(1321)*
   Si quis forte meam cupiet violare puellam, illum in desertis
     montibus urat Amor. *(1645)*
   Alliget hic curas, si quis obiurgat amantes et vetat assiduas
     currere fontis aquas. *(1649)*
   Quisquis amat, veniat. *(1824)*
   Nemo est bellus nisi qui amavit mulierem. *(1883)*
   Nam nemo flammas ustus amare potest. *(1898)*
   Vibius Restitutus hīc solus dormivit et Urbanam suam
     desiderabat. *(2146)*

4976. a reference to what was probably a prehistoric volcanic destruction
in Israel (see *Genesis* XVIII & XIX), a text probably written during the
eruption or even after by those first excavators of Pompeii, the Pompeians
1173. etc. qui = quisquis   bis...pereat: 'twice as much be damned'.   1883.
qui = is.

Serena Isidorum fastidat. *(3117)*

Nunc est ira recens, nunc est discedere tempus. Si dolor afuerit, crede, redibit amor. *(4491)*

Eutychis Graeca assibus II moribus bellis. *(4592)*

Cornelia Helena amatur a Rufō. *(4634)*

Quisquis amat, pereat. *(4659, 5186)*

Miximus in lectō; fateor, peccavimus, hospes. Si dicis quare, nulla matella fuit. *(4957)*

Restitutus multas decepit saepe puellas. *(5251)*

Sum tua aeris assibus II. *(5372)*

Si quis non vidit Venerem, quam pinxit Apelles, pupam meam aspiciat; talis et ille nitet. *(6842)*

Marcus Spendusam amat. *(7086)*

Amantes, ut apes, vitam mellitam exiguunt. *(8408)*

Venimus hoc cupidi, multo magis ire cupimus. *(8231, 10065)*

Rex es! *(10193a)*

c. for heroes and losers

Tetraites Prudens. Habeat Venerem Pompeianam, qui hoc laeserit. *(538)*

Epiphra! Pilicrepus non es! *(1926)*

4491. crede: sc. *mihi* 4592. assibus: the ablative of definite price again
4372. aeris: tells the metal of which the coin known as the *as* was made
6842. talis...nitet: 'even such a person as he (Apelles) would beam 7698b.
coniuge ab: reverse for translation — a bit of anastrophe 8408. a nice one
8231. An identical twin has been found at Herculaneum. hoc = huc.

Amianthus, Epaphra, Tertius ludunt cum Hedysiō. Iucundus Nolanus petat. Numerant Citus et Iacus Amianthus.
(1936)

Rusticus Malius, pugnarum XII, coronarum XI. *(4302)*

Thraex, Celadus, retiarius Crescens, puparum dominus.
(4356)

Thraex est suspirium puellarum. *(4397)*

Celadus, trium pugnarum, trium coronarum. *(4397)*

Acti, amor populi, cito redi! Vale! *(5395)*

Acti, domine scaenicorum, vale! *(5399)*

Oceanus libertus, victoriarum XIII, vicit, Aracinthus libertus, victoriarum IIII, periit. *(8055)*

Severus libertus, victoriarum XIII, periit; Albanus, Scari
libertus, victoriarum XIX, vicit. *(8056)*

Hermaissus invictus hactenus.

Popidio Rufo, invicto munerario III, (et) defensoribus
colonorum feliciter!

Paris, universus scaenae! scaenae domine, vale!

FROM THE SCRIPTORES

Anterus hoc scripsit. *(4925)*
Lucius pinxit. *(7535)*
III Kalendas Martias hīc scripsi. *(8729)*
Scripsi calamus cum atramentō. *(9127)*
Scripsit Celer — scripsit Aemilius Celer singulus ad lunam.

TEXTS THAT NAME A HOUSE (Casa Del Moralista)

Lascivos voltus et blandos aufer ocellos coniuge ab alterius.
Sit tibi in ore pudor!

Utere blanditiis odiosaque iurgia differ, si potes; aut gressus
ad tua tecta refer. *(7978)*

Abulat undā pedes puer et detergeat udos. Mappā torum
velet; lintea nostra cave.

1936. petat: sc. *eum (Hedysium)* as dir. obj. 5365. redi: imper. Acti:
vocative of a name universus: 'everyone's darling'.

DATES ON THE BOTTLES

Imperatore Vespasianō VII cos., IIII Idus Novembres ex fundō Sittiano imō, quem coluit Antonius Martialis ex dote *(5528)*

Faustō Corneliō (et) L. Salviō Othone cos., IIII Idus Apriles *(5512)*

Cossō Lentulō (et) M. Asiniō cos., Fundis. *(2552)*

Dolium I diffusum est Idibus Iuniis, L. Verginiō (et) C. Regulō cos. *(5519)*

C. Pomponiō (et) C. Aniciō cos., ex fundō Badianō diffusum Idibus Augusti bimum. *(2251, 5520)*

Ti. Catiō (et) P. Galeriō cos. *(9316)*

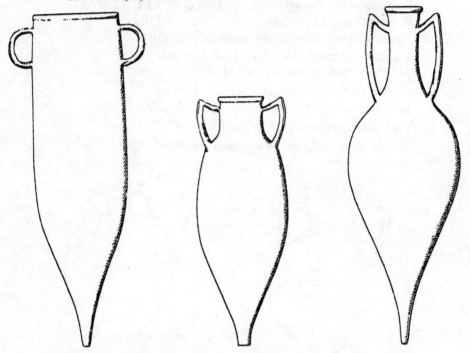

GENERAL NOTE ON THE VASA FICTILIA OF POMPEII: These items, brief though they are, are very significant in the economic life of the city and the vocabulary should be consulted carefully here.

5528ff. Great fun can be had with comparing brands & dates with the oinophile, Horace, in his *Odes.*

BRANDS OF WINE

M. Fabi Eupori Cnidum *(5535)*
Coum vetus P. Appulei Bassi *(5537)*
Coum, lectum ab Nicandrō Dorotheō *(5540)*
Choum vetus C. Atinio *(9320)*
Claudiae Trifolinum *(5570)*
Creticum excellens M. Stalabori Nymphodoti *(5526c)*
Surrentinum Fabianum, Imperatore Vespasianō IV cos. *(2556)*
Falernum Lucretianum, L. Cornuficiō cos. *(9313)*
Geminanum vinum *(5578)*
Marianum vinum *(5579)*
Nerone III cos., Murtites *(2554)*
Pompeianum vinum T. Vedio Vestali ab Castriciō *(5559)*
Rubrum vetus Vesuvianum picatum pondo CII *(2616)*
Rubrum vinum vetus annorum quatuor *(5597)*
Rubrum annorum quatuor Ampliato *(5660)*
Stabianum vinum Vedi Primigeni *(10310)*
Tauromenitanum vinum *(9333)*
Telesinum vetus annorum quatuor *(5569)*
Tironianum vinum vetus annorum V *(9333)*
Vinum rubrum in usus Coeliae Proculae *(9362)*
Vinum vetus mulsum, Domitiano cos. III *(5526a)*

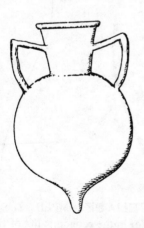 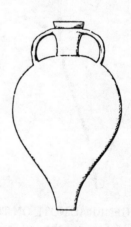

5535. Cnidum: sc. *vinum,* as thruout here.   A Further Note:
Names pour all thru the breakables, and sometimes they are the names of
owners of houses that have been excavated. Here one sees the real ancient
world of everyday life. Note the preponderance of Greek names amongst
the slaves who ran much of the economic life of Pompeii.

OTHER PRODUCTS CONTAINED

Garum factum per se ex officinā Scauri *(2572)*
Garum, flos scombi, Scauri ab Eutyche, Scauri servō *(2576)*
Garum castum Scombri Fortunati *(5662)*
Gari flos *(5663)*
Garum, flos Murenae Salusti *(5673)*
Garum, flos scombri optimi, ex officinā Agathopi *(5690)*
Gari flos ab Tinniō Restitutō *(10271)*
Gustaticium *(5589)*
Hallex optima Vibiae *(9411)*

Limense vetus annorum VII rubrum *(2585)*
Liquamen A. Umbrici Scauri *(2587, 5710)*
Liquamen optimum *(2589, 2590, 2591, 2593, 5706)*
Liquamen optimum A. Virnio Modesto ab Agathopode
Lomentum *(2592)*
Lomentum Gaviae Severae *(5737)*
Lympha vetus annorum IIII M. Valeri Heliadis *(9377a)*
Mel Thyminum imum Gaviae Severae *(5741)*
Mel Corsicum pondo II *(10288)*
Mulsum *(5526, 5527, 5592)*

Muriae flos ab Umbriciā *(5723)*
Muria casta
Ab Apuleiō Verō nuces mille *(5671)*
Olivae albae dulces *(2610)*
Olivas M. Ampliati *(5762)*
Oliva alba P. Tegeti *(9437)*
Olivas ex aquā *(10292)*
Oleum *(9435)*
Passum Rhodium P. Coeli Galli *(9327)*
Piper *(5763)*

ΚΛΛΙΚ

DRAMATIS PERSONAE

M. Stlabori Felicis *(2665)*
Albucio Celso *(5768)*
M. Amulli Hermeti *(5772)*

10292. ex = in 2665ff. watch cases to give trans. of "for" or "of".

C. Annio Maximo *(5773)*
M. C. Iusti *(5786)*
Caesiae Helpidi *(5791a)*
Claudio, Trophimi servo *(5811)*
Caecilio Iucundo ab Sexstō Metellō

MISCELLANY

Onesimus fecit. *(2777)*
XII Kalendas Octobres apertum est. *(5531a)*
XII Idus Decembres ab Hermete vinae amphora aperta. *(5532)*
Clodianum vetus annorum III P. Clodi Sperati Suedi. Clemens, vale feliciter! *(5574)*
Defrutum excellens C. Antoni Rustici, confectum a servō Fortunatō. *(5585)*
Epaphrodi sum; tangere me noli. *(6251)*
Fur, cave malum! *(6253)*
Redde me! *(6260)*
P. Cornelius, Corinti servōs, fecit. *(9683)*
Amphoram Romanus fecit in figulinis Thesmi Surrentini. *(10392)*

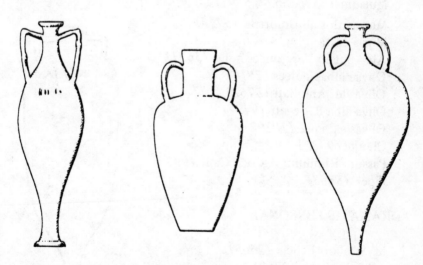

2777. Onesimus: a runaway slave with this name caused St. Paul to write his *Epistle to Philemon,* the shortest Pauline epistle in the New Testament 5532. aperta: sc. *est.* GENERAL NOTE: sum + personal name: 'I belong to' 6251. noli tangere: the correct negative of the imperative

THE POTS AND PANS OF POMPEII

JARS *(8047)*

    A. Appulei Hilaronis. Firmus fecit. *(3)*
    Asclepiadis Ponti *(5)*
    Phileros, M. Fulvi servus *(15)*

BASINS *(8048)*

    Cn. Domitius Secundus fecit. *(18)*
    T. Iulius Iucundus fecit. *(19)*
    M. Marius Priscus fecit. *(24)*
    M. Marius Secundus fecit. *(25)*
    T. Tettius restituit. *(45)*

LAMPS *(8052)*

    Annum novum faustum felicem! *(1)*

DISHES BIG AND SMALL *(8055)*

    Epaphroditi sum; tangere me noli *(14)*
    Germani officina *(20)*
    C. Petroni Saturni *(31)*
    Sabinus fecit. *(39)*
    Vateri officina *(43)*
    Villi Natalis *(44)*
    Redde me! *(58)*

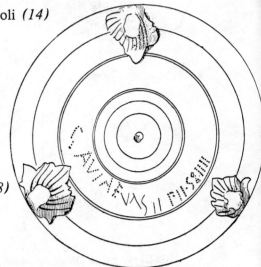

SEALS *(8058)*

    Celeris, Q. Grani Veri servi *(18)*
    P. Viselli *(94)*
    Q. Octavi Romuli *(60)*
    N. Popidi Prisci *(70)*

WEIGHTS *(8067)*

Ti. Claudiō Caesare Augustō IIII, L. Vitelliō III cos., pondera exacta, M. Articuleiō (et) Cn. Turrancō aedilibus. *(1)*
Fur, cave malum! *(6)*
Philoxenus libertus aedituus Laribus familiaribus donum dedit. *(12)*

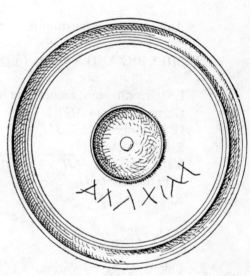

TOKENS *(8069)*

A. Iuni Perennis *(116)*

HOUSEHOLD UTENSILS *(8071)*·

Corelia Nymphe aurum pondo XX *(1)*
C. Sesti Zosimi *(14)*
C. Calpurnia Romae fecit *(32)*

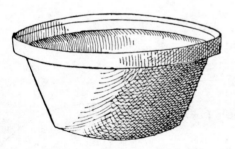

8052.1 ye exclamatory acc. again   8071.1 pondo: indeclinable. 32.
Romae: one more locative.

FROM THE STREET OF THE TOMBS

on the boundary stones by the Herculaneum and Nuceria
Gates:

Ex auctoritate Imperatoris Caesaris Vespasiani Augusti loca
publica a privatis possessa T. Suedius Clemens tribunus, causis
cognitis et mensuris factis, reipublicae Pompeianorum restituit.
(1018)

from Group I, by the Herculaneum Gate:

M. Cerrinius Restitutus, Augustalis. Locus datus est decuri-
onum decretō. *(994)*
A. Veio, Marci filio, IIviro iure dicundō iterum, quinquennali,
tribuno militum, ab populō ex decurionum decretō. *(996)*
M. Porci, Marci fili, ex decurionum decretō in frontem pedes
XXV, in agrum pedes XXV. *(997)*
Mamiae, Publici filiae, sacerdoti publicae locus sepulturae
datus decurionum decretō. *(998)*
Istacidia, Numerii filia, Rufilla, sacerdos publica. *(999)*

from Group III further up on the left:

A. Umbrico, Auli filio, Meneniā Scauro, duumviro iure dicundō. Huic decuriones locum monumenti et HS ∞∞ in funere
et statuam equestrem in Forō ponendum censuerunt. Scaurus
pater filio. *(1024)*
C. Calventio Quieto, Augustali. Huic ob munificentiam
decurionum decretō et populi consensū biselii honor datus est.
(1026)

1018. a copy of this stone, of which there were several around the city,
when found in the 18th century, determined which city was being uncovered. The stone was set up after a land issue in which the Emperor was
involved. reipublicae: here 'city' GENERAL NOTE: With these sepulchral
texts should be compared Trimalchio's as given in the *Cena Trimalchionis*
of Petronius; watch the formulae thruout which can be paralleled on the
Via Appia outside Rome 997. agrum: 'breadth', from its original meaning
998. datus: sc.*est* 1024. Meneniā: an abl. of source tucked into the name
'of the Menenian tribe' ponendum: 'to be erected'.

Naevolia, Luci liberta, Tyche sibi et C. Nunatio Fausto, Augustali et pagano, cui decuriones consensu populi bisellium ob merita eius decrevit. Hoc monumentum Naevolia Tyche libertis suis libertabusque et C. Munati Fausti viva fecit. *(1030)*

from Group II

T. Terentio, Titi filio, Menenia Felici Maiori, aedili. Huic publice locus datus est et HS ∞∞. Fabia, Probi filia, Sabina uxor. *(1019)*

from Group IV further on up the right:

M. Alleio Luccio, Libellae patri, aedili, duumviro, praefecto, quinquennali, et M. Alleio, Libellae filio, decurioni. Vixit annis XVII. Locus monumenti publice datus est. Alleia, Marci filia, Decimilla, sacerdos publica Cereris, faciundum curavit viro et filio. *(1036)*

L. Ceio, Luci filio, Menenia, Labeoni, iterum duumviro iure dicundo, quinquennali, Menomachus libertus. *(1037)*

Salvius puer vixit annis VI. *(1032)*

Numerio Velasio Grato. Vixit annos XII. *(1041)*

M. Arrius, Cai libertus, Diomedes sibi (et) suis memoriae magister pagi Augusti Felicis suburbani. *(1042)*

Arriae, Marci filliae, Diomedes libertus (et) sibi (et) suis. *(1043)*

from near the Stabian Gate:

L. Avianius, Luci filius, Menenia, Flaccus Pontianus (et) Q. Spadius, Quinti filius, Menenia, Firmus, duoviri iure dicundo, viam a milliario ad cisiarios, qua territorium est Pompeianorum, sua pecunia munierunt. *(1064)*

1030. decrevit: the town-councillors, who formed the town-council are considered a single unit sc. *libertis libertabusque* before *C. Munati Fausti*
1036. faciundum (*esse*): sc. *hoc monumentum.*
1037. iterum: an unusual position sc. *hoc monumentum fecit* 1032. annis: a spelling error here 1042. Suis: 'for his own people'. memoriae: 'of (happy) memory 1064. ad: 'near'. qua: 'where'. munierunt = muniverunt, as usual.

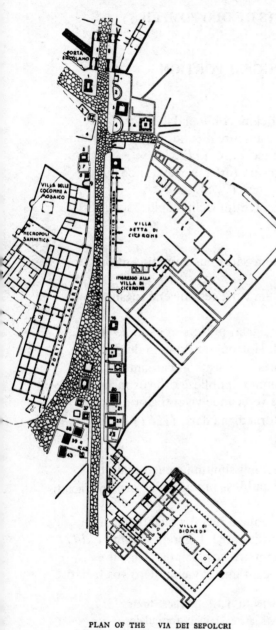

PLAN OF THE VIA DEI SEPOLCRI

A. HERCULANEUM GATE.
B. CITY WALL.
D. ROAD ALONG CITY WALL.
E - E. VESUVIUS ROAD.

1 - 9. TOMBS – GROUP II.
   1. Tomb without a name.
   2. Sepulchral enclosure of Terentius Felix.
   3, 4. Tombs without names.
   5. Sepulchral enclosure
   6. Garland tomb.
   7. Sepulchral enclosure.
   8. Tomb of the Blue Glass Vase.
   9. Sepulchral niche.

10 - 30. VILLA.
   10, 11, 13, 14. Shops
   12. Garden belonging to Tombs 8 and 9.
   15. Street entrance of Inn.
   16-28. Rooms belonging to the Inn.
   29-30. Potter's establishment.

31 - 32. SAMNITE GRAVES.

33 - 43. TOMBS – GROUP IV.
   33. Unfinished tomb.
   34. Tomb with the marble door.
   35. Unfinished tomb.
   36. Sepulchral enclosure with small pyramids.
   37. Tomb of Luccius Libella.
   38. Tomb of Ceius Labeo.
   39. Tomb without a name.
   40. Sepulchral niche of Salvius.
   41. Sepulchral niche of Velasius Gratus.
   42. Tomb of M. Arrius Diomedes.
   43. Tomb of Arria.

37

THE PAINTED TEXTS OF OLD POMPEII

ELECTORAL BILLS – THE BIGGEST PORTION

a. for Proculus

Procule, Frontoni tuo officium commenda! *(920)*

P. Paquium Proculum IIvirum iure dicundo dignum rēpublicā universi Pompeiani fecerunt. *(1122)*

Aedilem Proculum cunctorum turba probavit; hoc pudor
ingenuus postulat et pietas. *(7065)*

P. Paquium Proculum duumvirum vicini cupidi faciunt.

b. for Pansa

C. Cuspium Pansam aedilem Saturnius cum discentibus
rogat. *(275)*

C. Cuspium Pansam aedilem aurifices universi rogant.
(710)

Cuspium Pansam aedilem lignari universi rogant. *(960)*

C. Gavium Rufum (et) M. Holconium Priscum duoviros
iure dicundo orō vos faciatis. Cuspium Pansam Popidium
Secundum aedilem dignum reipublicae oro vos faciatis. *(2292)*

Cuspium aedilem! Si qua verecunde viventi gloria danda
est, huic iuveni debet gloria digna dari. *(7201)*

c. for Vettius

A. Vettium Firmum, verecundissimum iuvenem, duumvirum viis aedibus sacris publicis procurandis, oro vos faciatis.
(456)

Aulum Vettium Firmum aedilem oro vos faciatis, dignum
rēpublicā virum! Oro vos faciatis! Pilicrepi, facite! *(1147)*

A. Vettium Firmum aedilem oro vos faciatis. Dignus est.
Caprasia cum Nymphiō rogant una et vicini. Oro vos faciatis!

GENERAL NOTE ON THE ELECTION NOTICES: These texts,
the largest chunk of the surviving texts, are extremely formulaic
and most follow a predicatble pattern. Help is given only once.
920. officium: 'vote' 1122. republica: abl. with *dignum* we see all stages
of Proculus' election 710. aurifices: These electoral texts are most helpful
in showing the chronic life of the city 2292. This is the usual form, even
if *dignum* has a dative to complete its meaning! 7201. qua = aliqua. verecunde viventi: sc. *viro*.

38

d. for Trebius
  Trebium aedilem oro vos faciatis. Clibanari rogant. *(677)*
  Trebium aedilem tonsorem! *(743)*
  Trebi, surge; fac aedilem Lollium Fuscum, adulescentem
    probum! *(7619)*

e. for Sabinus
  Cn. Helvium Sabinum aedilem Isiaci universi rogant. *(787)*
  Cn. Helvium Sabinum aedilem aliari rogant. *(3485)*
  Cn. Helvium Sabinum aedilem pistores rogant et cupiunt
    cum vicinis. *(7273)*
  Cn. Helvium Sabinum aedilem Maria rogat. *(7866)*
  Valeas, dormis; dormis et cupis; Trebi, surge; fac Helvium
    Sabinum aedilem; dormis.

f. for Popidius .
  Popidium Secundum aedilem dignum reipublicae, probis-
    simum iuvenem, oro vos faciatis. Rufine, fave et ille te
    faciet. *(3409)*
  L. Popidium aedilem Ismurna rogat. *(7221)*
  Popidium IIvirum! Graphice, vigila! *(7649)*
  L. Popidium iuvenem aedilem! Crescens, scio te cupere.
    (7910)

g. for another Sabinus
  M. Epidium Sabinum aedilem Campanienses rogant. *(470)*
  Sabinum aedilem, Procule, et ille te faciet. *(635)*
  Sabinum et Rufum aediles, dignos reipublicae, Valentinus
    cum †discentes† suos rogat. *(698)*
  M. Epidium Sabinum duumvirum dicundō iure oro vos
    faciatis; dignus est; defensorem coloniae ex sententiā Suedi
    Clementis, sancti iudicis, consensū ordinis ob merita eius et
    probitatem dignam reipublicae faciatis. Sabinus signator cum
    plausū facit. *(768)*

---

743. The exclamatory accusative! Consult the vocabulary to find out just
what these offices meant in the city government   3409. sc. *ei* as obj. of *fave*
698. suos: in his haste the sign-painter (*scriptor*) put the objects of the prep.
cum in the wrong case   768. faciatis: *oro Sabinum* must be supplied; note
the scriptor getting the last word; Suedius Clemens was the Emperor's judge
who settled the land problem around the walls of the city.

M. Epidium Sabinum IIvirum iure dicundō oro vos faciatis, dignum iuvenum. Suedius Clemens sanctissimus iudex
fecit, vicinis rogantibus. *(787)*
M. Epidium Sabinum IIvirum iure dicundō oro vos faciatis.
Trebius Clemens facit, consentiente sanctissimō ordine. *(2605)*

h. for Polybius
C. Iulium Polybium IIvirum muliones rogant. *(113)*
C. Iulium Polybium IIvirum Vatia rogat. *(172)*
C. Iulium Polybium aedilem oro vos faciatis. Panem
  bonam fert. *(429)*
C. Iulium Polybium! Lanternari, tene scalam! *(7621)*

i. miscellaneous
M. Marium aedilem faciatis rogo vos. *(3)*
P. Furium IIvirum, virum bonum, oro vos faciatis. *(67)*
M. Holconium Priscum IIvirum iure dicundo! *(157)*
Casellium aedilem! *(223)*
Herennium Celsum aedilem oro vos faciatis! *(299)*
Ti. Claudium Verum IIvirum vicini rogant. *(367,522a)*
Claudium IIvirum animula facit. *(425)*
Communem nummum dividendum censio est. Nam
  noster Nummus magnam habet pecuniam. *(1597)*
Bruttium Balbum IIvirum Genialis rogat. Hic aerarium
  conservabit. *(3702)*
Ampliatum, Luci filium, aedilem, vicini, surgite et rogate!
  Lutati, fac! *(7447)*
Ordini decurionum feliciter! M. Satrio liberis reipublicae
  bene merentibus iurenes rogamus. *(7687)*

j. parodies
Vatiam aedilem rogant Marerio (et) dormientes universi.
  (575)
Vatiam aedilem furunculi rogant. *(576)*
M. Cerrinum Vatiam aedilem oro vos. Seribibi universi
rogant. Scribunt Florus cum Frontō. *(581)*
Montanus cliens rogat cum latruncularis. *(7851)*

1597. censio est: 'there is a motion that'. dividendum: sc. *esse.* Nummus:
a man's name and the name of a Roman coin 7687. liberis: sc. *et* before
this word 581. scribunt: Florus cum Frontō adds up to a plural in the
mind of the Pompeiian writer

ANNOUNCEMENTS OF GAMES

Cnaei Allei Nigidi Mai quinquennalis gladiatorum paria XXX et eorum suppositici pugnabunt Pompeiis VIII, VI, V Kalendis Decembres. Venatio erit. Maio quinquennali feliciter! Paris, vale! *(1179)*

Lucreti Valentis, flaminis Neronis Augusti, fili Perpetui, D. Lucreti Valentis fili, familia gladiatoria pugnabit Pompeiis V Kalendas Apriles; venatio et vale erunt. *(1185)*

A. Suetti Certi aedilis familia gladiatorum pugnabit Pompeiis pridie Kalendas Iunias; venatio et vale erunt. Omnibus Neronis funeribus feliciter! *(1190)*

Hīc venatio pugnabit V. Kalendas Septembres et Felix ad ursos pugnabit. *(1989)*

Decimi Lucreti Satri Valentis, flaminis Neronis Caesaris Augusti, fili Perpetui, gladiatorum paria X et Decimi Lucreti fili gladiatorum paria X pugnabunt Pompeiis VI, V, IV, III, pridie Idus Apriles. Venatio legitima et vela erunt. Scribit Aemilius Celer singulus ad lunam. *(3884)*

Pro salute Neronis Claudi Caesaris Augusti Germanici Pompeiis Tiberi Claudi Veri venatio, athletae, et sparsiones erunt V, IIII Kalendas Martias. *(7989)*

Dedicatione operis tabularum gladiatores Cn. Allei Nigidi Mai pugnabunt Pompeiis Idibus Iunis. Pompa, venatio, athletae, vela erunt. Ocella scripsit. Nigra, vale! *(7993)*

Paria XLIV familia Capiniana muneribus Augustorum pugnabunt Puteolis ante diem IV Idus Maias, pridie Idus Maias et XVII, XV Kalendas Iunias. Vela erunt. Magus scripsit. *(7994)*

A GENERAL NOTE ON THE PROGRAMMATA: these again are formulaic and help will be given in the notes only once; for calendar knowledge consult Appendix V.

1179. paria: 'pairs' or companies owned by men like baseball clubs today 1989. pugnabit: 'will occur'. ad = contra 3884. ad: by 7993. operis tabularum: 'treasury building 7994. Puteolis: see map.

SELECTED TABLETS OF LUCIUS CAECILIUS IUCUNDUS

The most important evidence relating to private business transactions in the ancient world are the receipts, discovered in 1875, which formed a part of the private accounts of Lucius Caecilius Jucundus. Jucundus lived on the Via di Stabia (see map). In the atrium of his house was found a pair of matching herms, one of which is in the Museo Nazionale in Naples. The bust of bronze is modeled "with realistic vigor. There is no attempt to soften the prominent features. We see the Pompeian auctioneer just as he was: a shrewd, alert, energetic man with somewhat of a taste for art and more for the good things of life — a man who would bear watching in a financial transaction." So Jucundus is described by Mau in his standard work, *Pompeii*.

The receipts were written on wax tablets, which were carefully packed in a wooden box. The box, which was on the second storey of the house, crumbled to pieces when the volcanic dust was removed; but 153 tablets kept their shape and were taken to the Naples Museum. The wood had turned to charcoal because of the intense heat during the eruption. However, this heat preserved the tablets (as it did many wooden beams and even doors — especially in Herculaneum), and the writing was so clear on them (see the illustrations) that Zangemeister was able to edit them for the *Corpus Inscriptionum Latinarum* in 1895 as a separate supplementary volume to the buried cities' graffiti in Volume IV. They had first been edited by De Petra in Rome in 1876.

One tablet dates from 15 AD, another from 27, all the others range from 52 to 62. Most of the tablets are made up of three leaves, 5" high by 2" to 4" wide, thus providing six pages. Pages I and VI served as covers. Pages II and III were devoted to the actual receipt. After the receipt had been made up, the first two leaves were brought together and tied by a thread, whose ends met in the broad groove down the middle of page IV. Wax seals were made along the thread by the witnesses, who then signed their names alongside their seals. Many of these still survive. A memorandum was placed on page V. Only the receipts were legally binding.

Nearly all the tablets record transactions connected with auction sales, the person whose effects were thus disposed of giving Jucundus a recipt in full for the proceeds of the sale less a commission. A few contain receipts for rent which Jucundus paid for the use of property belonging to the City: a fullery, a pasture, and a plowfield. There are those also which note the loans he made and the purchasing of Egyptian linen. On the following pages are presented a few of these *tabulae ceretae,* as they are known, giving the actual receipt and the accompanying memorandum. Needless to say, a vivid mental picture of Lucius Caecilius Jucundus of Pompeii will emerge.

"Shrewd and secure, he had let the sculptor display a true likeness with great flapping ears and a large wart and a shrewd smile behind which one can see him adding up the interest and compounding it. He filled his house with the beauty his money could buy — frescoes and exquisitely worked silver utensils. He was equally scrupulous with his accounts, noting down his transactions upon 154 waxed tablets." — *Life,* March 25, 1966.

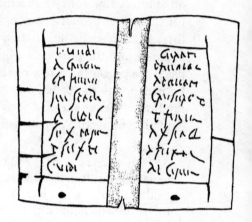

I. A Unique Tablet *(2)*

Receipt: HS n(ummos) DXX ob mulum venditum M. Pompo-
nio, M(arci) l(iberto), Niconi, quam pequniam in stipulatum L.
Caecili Felicis redegisse dicitur M. Cerrinius Euprates. Eam
pecuniam omnem, quae supra scripta est, nummeratum dixit
se accepisse M. Cerrinius, M(arci) l(iberus), Euphrates ab Phila-
delphō, Caecili Felicis ser(vō).
Actum Pompeis V K(alendas) Iunias, Drusō Caesare (et) C.   15 AD
Norbanō Flaccō cos.   *(1)*

II. Several Auction Tablets *(2 - 137)*

Receipt: HS n(ummos)   CCC, quae pecunia in stipulatum L.
Caecili Iucundi venit ob auctionem M. Allei Crispi in Idus De-
cembr(es) primas, mercede minus numeratā,habere se dixit
M. Alleius Carpus ab L. Caeciliō Iucundō.
Act(um) Pomp(eis) V K(alendas) Dec(embres), L. Calpurniō
(et) M. Liciniō cos.   *(2)*   27 AD

Receipt: HS n(ummos) "I" XXXVIIII, quae pecunia in stipulatum L. Caecili Iucundi venit ob auctionem Umbriciae Ianu-
ariae, mercede minus persolutā, habere se dixsit Umbricia Ianu-
aria ab L. Caeciliō Iucundō.
Act(um) Pomp(eis) pri(die) Id(us) Dec(embres), L. Duviō (et)   56 AD
P. Clodiō cos.
Memorandum: I. Duviō Avitō (et) P. Clodiō Thraseā consulibus, pr(idie) Id(us) Decembres, D. Volcius Thallus scripsi rogatū Umbriciae eam accepisse ab L. Caeciliō Iucundō HS

GENERAL NOTE: The language of the tablets is extremely formulaic and
thus items noted will probably re-appear; for calendar matters you are referred to Appendix V.

#1. HS: the equivalent of our $. Niconi: with *M. Pomponio.* pequniam:
archaism. in stipulatum: 'in agreement with'. nummos: 'in cash', as with
numeratus below. cos: the extremely common abbreviation for *consulibus*
#2. mercede minus: 'with the handling fee deducted'. ∞: the numeral usu-
ally written as M

n(ummos) $\overline{XI}$ XXXIX ex auctione eius, mercede minus, ex interrogatione factā tabellarum. A(ctum Pompe)is. *(25)*

Receipt: HS n(ummos) ((1)) LXXXV, quae pecunia in stipulatu(m) venit L. Caeci(li) Iucundi ob auctionem buxiariam C. Iuli Onesimi in Idus Iulias primas, mercede minus, numeratos accepisse dixit C. Iulius Onesimus ab M. Fabiō Agathinō nomine L. Caecili Iucundi.
Actum Pompeis VI Idus Maias, M'. Aciliō Aviolā (et) M. Asiniō Marcellō cos.   *(5)*   54 AD

Receipt: L. Duviō Avitō (et) P. Clodiō cos., IIII Idus Decem-   56 AD
br(es) M. Helvius Catullus scripsi rogatū Umbriciae Antiochidis eam accepisse ab L. Caecilio Iucundo HS $\overline{VI}$ CCLII nummos ob auctionem Trophimi, servi eius, mercede minus. Act(um) Pom-(peis). Memorandum: L. Duviō (et) P. Clodiō cos., IIII Idus Dece(mbres) M. Helvius Catullus scripsi rogatu Umbriciae eam accepis(se) ab Iucundo HS n(ummos) $\overline{VI}$ CCLII ob auctionem Trophim(i), servi eius, mercede min(us). Act(um) Pomp(eis).
(24)

Receipt: Nerone Caesare II (et) L. Calpurniō cos., VII K(alen-   57 AD
das) Februarias. Ti. Claudius Syn . . . scripsi rogatū et mandatū Abscanti Caesaris Aug(usti) Philippiani eum accepisse ab L. Caeciliō Iucundō sestertia duo milia septingentos triginta duos nummos . . . Act(um) Pomp(eis).
Memorandum: Nerone Caesare II (et) L. Calpurniō cos., VII K(alendas) Febr(uarias) Ti. Claudius Syn . . . scripsi rogatū et mandatū Abscanti Caesaris Augusti Philippiani eum accepisse ab L. Caeciliō Iucundō HS n(ummos)∘∘ DCCXXXII. . .
Act(um Pompeis).   *(30)*

Receipt: M'. Aciliō Aviolā (et) M. Asiniō cos., IIII K(alendas)   54 AD
Iunias Salvius, heredum N. Nasenni (et) Nigidi Vacculae servōs scripsi me accepisse ab L. Caeciliō Iucundō sestertia nummum

---

#25. ((1)): a short-hand form of 10,000. mercede minus persoluta: the fuller form of *mercede minus.* $\overline{XI}$: the bar multiplies the number by 1000. ex: 'according to' #24. The position of women in Roman imperial society was hardly subservient #30. Some fire damage here. Caesaris Augusti: one should not be entirely surprised to see the imperial name coming up at Pompeii as Nero's Empress's family hailed from here and slaves often (as in America with George Washington Carver) take their names from heroes.

tria millia quinquaginta Nove(m) nummos ob auctione(m) mea(m),
quem in stipulatu(m) eius redegi; quae minutati(m) quem ad modum volui ab eō accepi in hanc diem. Actum Pompeis. *(6)*

III. The Rent Receipts

a. for estates *(138-40)*

Receipt: Q. Coeliō Caltiliō Iustō (et) L. Heviō Blaesiō Proculō
IIvir(is) iur(e) d(icundō), pri(die) Idus Martias Secundus, colo-
norum coloniae Veneriae Corneliae servōs, accepi P. Terentiō
Primō HS DCCLXXXVI ob avitum et patritum fundi reliquos
Audiani nomine Stali Inventi iussū Caltili Iusti et Halvi Proculi.
Act(um) Pomp(eis), D. Iuniō Torquatō Silanō (et) Q. Hateriō   53 AD
Antoniō cos.
Memorandum: Q. Coeliō Caltiliō Iustō (et) L. Helviō Blaesiō
Proculō, IIvir(is) i(ure) d(icundō), pr(idie) Idus Mart(ias) Se-
cundus, c(olonorum) c(oloniae) V(eneriae) C(orneliae) ser(vōs),
scripsi me accepisse ab P. Terentiō Primō HS DCCLXXVI reli-
quos ob avitum fundi Audiani et accepi ante hanc diem HS V
CCXXIIII. Act(um) Pompeis, D. Iuniō Silanō (et) Q. Hateriō
Antoninō cos.   *(138)*

b. rents from fullers *(141-44)*

Receipt: Sex. Pompeiō Proculō (et) C. Corneliō Marcō IIvi(ris)
i(ure) d(icundō), XI K(alendas) Mart(ias) Privatus, coloniae
ser(vus), scripsi me accepisse ab L. Caeciliō Iucundō sestertios
mille sescentos quinquaginta duo nummos ob fullonicam ex
reliquis anni unius.
Act(um) Pom(peis), Nerone Aug(ustō) III (et) M. Messallā cos.   58 AD
Memorandum: Sex. Pompeō Proculō (et) C. Corneliō Marcō
d(uumviris) i(ure) d(icundō), XI K(alendas) Mart(ias) Privatus
colonor(um) colon(iae) se(rvus), scripsi me accepisse ab L.
Caecil(iō) Iucund(ō) HS ○ DCII ob fullon(icam) ex reliq(uis)
ann(i) un(ius). Nerone Caes(are) III (et) Messallā cos. *(141)*

#6. servos: the old nominative singular for *servus.* nummum: omit in
trans. quem ad modum: 'as' #138. IIviris = duoviris, 'mayors'. ob...
Audiani: 'for the rent of the Audian estate of his father and grandfather'.
colonorum...servos: 'servant of the colonists of the colony of Venus &
Sulla' — a long-winded way of saying 'of the city of Pompeii' as Venus was
the tutelary deity and Sulla its patron #141. reliquis: 'the rents.'

Receipt: Cn. Pompeiō Grosphō (et) Grosphō Pompeiō Gavianō
IIvir(is) iur(e) dic(undō), VI Idus Iulias Privatus, colonorum
coloniae Veneriae Corneliae Pompeianorum ser(vus), scripsi
me accepisse ab L. Caeciliō Iucundō sestertios mille sescentos
quinquaginta nummos nummō (et) libellas quinque ex reliquis
ob fullonicam anni L. Verani Hupsaci et Albuci Iusti, d(uum)-
v(irorum) i(ure) d(icundō).
Memorandum: Duobus Grosphic d(uumviris) i(ure) d(icundō),
VI Idus Iulias chirographum Privati, c(olonorum) c(oloniae)
V(enteriae) C(orneliae) s(ervi); HS   DCLIS ob fullonicam anni
terti, duobus Grosphis d(uum)v(iris) i(ure) d(icundō). T. Sex-
tiō (et) M. Osturiō cos.   *(143)*

   c. rents from pastures *(145-47)*

Receipt: C. Corneliō Macrō (et) Sex. Pompeiō Proculō duumviris i(ure) d(icundō), Nonis Ianuaris Privatus, coloniae, Pom-
peianor(um) ser(vus), scripsi me accepisse ab. L. Caeciliō Iucundō
sestertia duo millia sescentos septuaginta quinque nummos ex
reliquis ob pasqua anni Modesti et Vibi Secundi, IIvir(orum)
i(ure) d(icundō).
Act(um) Pom(peis), Nerone Caesare III(et) M. Messallā Cor-
vinō cos.
Memorandum: C. Corneliō Macrō (et) Sex. Pom(peiō) Proculō
d(uumviris) i(ure) d(icundō), Nonis Ianuariis Privatus, colon-
or(um) Pompeianor(um) ser(vus), scripsi me accepisse ab L.
Caecili(ō) Iucundō HS   DCLXXV et reliquis ob pascua anni
Modesti et Vibi Secundi.
Act(um) Pom(peis), Nerone Caesare III (et) M. Messallā Cor-
vin(o) c(os.).   *(145)*

Receipt: L. Veraniō Hupsaeō (et) L. Albuciō Iustō duumviris
iure dic(undō), XIII K(alendas) Iulias Privatus, coloniae Pom-
peian(orum) ser(vus), scripsi me accepisse ab L. Caeciliō Iucundō sestertios mille sescentos septuaginta quinque nummos
et accepi ante hanc diem (quae dies fuit VIII Idus Iunias) sester-
(tios) mille nummos ob vectigal publicum pasqua.
Act(um) Pom(peis), Cn. Fonteiō (et) C. Vipstanō cos.

#143. nummos nummo: 'all in cold, hard cash'. chirographum: sc. *hoc
est* for a full sentence. HS: with the amount supply *soluta sunt* as main
verb.

Memorandum: L. Veranio Hupsaō (et) L. Albuciō Iustō d(uumviris) i(ure) d(icundo) XIV K(alendas) Iul(ias) Privatus, c(olonorum) c(oloniae) V(eneriae) C(orneliae) ser(vus), scripsi me
accepisse ab L. Caecilio Iucundo HS ∞ DCLXXV et accepi
ante hanc diem, VIII Idus Iunias, HS∞ num(mos) ob vextigal
publicu(m) pasquorum.
Act(um) Pom(peis), C. Fonteiō (et) C. Vipstanō cos.   *(147)*

d. a credit note *(148-53)*

Receipt: L. C. . . (et) Ti. Claudiō Verō, d(uumviris) i(ure)
d(icundō), III Idus Ianuarias Privatus, colon(iae) Pompeian-
(orum) ser(vus), scripsi me accepisse ab L. Caeciliō Iucundō
sestertia duo millia quingentos viginti numm(os) nomine M.
Fabi Agathini, mancipis mercatūs.
Act(um) Pom(peis), P. Mariō, P(ubli) f(iliō), (et) L. Afiniō cos.
(151)

#145. III: 'for the third time' #147. publicum pasqua: the public scribe
did not always spell or inflect his nouns carefully as he should have written
publicorum pascuorum. vextigal - vectigal. publicum = public(or)um, a
contraction frequently used in poetry #151. mercatūs; 'for the market'.

THE OTHER TEXTS OF LUCIUS CAECILIUS IUCUNDUS

It would not be at all surprising to find a rich and influential man like our Pompeian banker appearing in other texts at Pompeii, amongst the graffiti and/or the formal texts of the city. The logical and substantiated starting point for the search would be his house on lot XXVI in Block I of Ward V, where the tablets were discovered. The home itself, excavated in 1875, is a treasure house. Its dining-room (*tablinum*) contains what August Mau termed one of the most beautiful specimens of ancient painting: a part of a fresco showing Hector's return to Troy after ransoming his son's body from the Greeks. The shrine for the household gods (*lararium*) is invaluable with its marble reliefs showing the Forum and a gate-tower in the throes of the earthquake of 63 — the harbinger none comprehended. However, upon entry into the house today one is immediately drawn to the far side of the reception-room (*atrium*) with its entrance leading to the living-area (*peristylium*). On either side of the door are two marble shafts, both to be surmounted by a bust of the banker with most realistic vigor right down to the wart on his chin. The surviving bust on the visitor's left is a copy of the original in the Museo Nazionale in Naples. The first descriptions of Jucundus' House and Tablets will be found in Appendix IV.

On the marble shaft below Jucundus' bust:

> Genio Luci nostri Felix libertus.   *(860)*

On a column in the peristyle of Jucundus' house:

> Staphilus hīc cum Quietā. *(4087)*

On a wine bottle in the house of Jucundus:

> Caecilio Iucundo ab Sexstō Metellō. *(5788)*

---

860. genio: 'innate goodness'. for a main verb we require something like HOC SIGNUM DEDICAVIT 4087. for a main verb ERAT is fine.

An election notice mentioning Jucundus' two sons:

> Ceium Secundum IIvirum Quintus (et) Sextus Caecili
> Iucundi rogant. *(3433)*

On a wine bottle found in Herculaneum:

> Caecilio Iucundo. *(10768)*

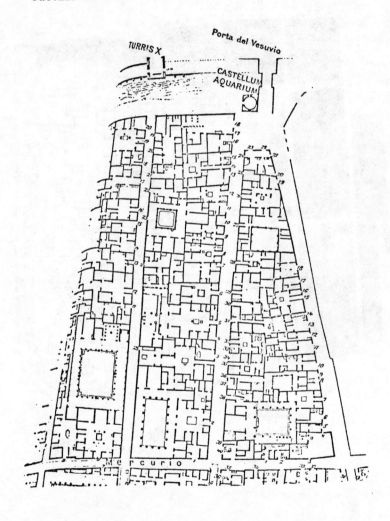

3344. Caecilii Iucundi: plural since the two brothers, Quintus & Sextus,
are making the request.

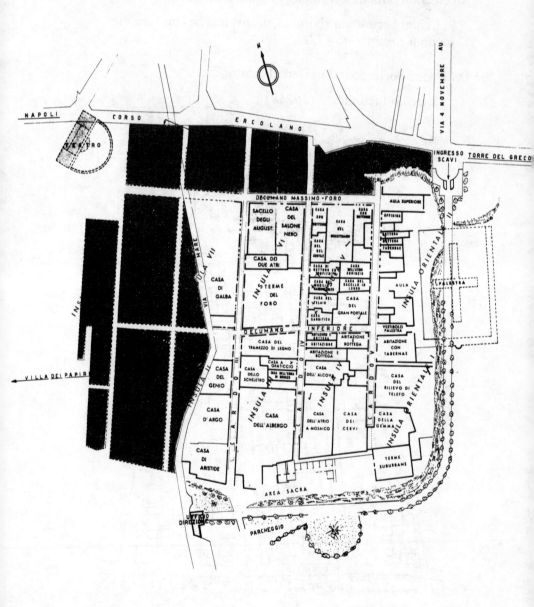

52

AN ALBUM OF INSCRIPTIONS FROM HERCULANEUM

Herculaneum was the first of the cities of Vesuvius to be discovered and excavated, but its excavation has been highly irregular. And yet Herculaneum was the key to Pompeii. Herculaneum was not known until a resident of Resina (the modern town built right over the ancient city, now renamed Ercolano) attempted to dig his well deeper in 1710 (onto the stage of Herculaneum's theatre as it turned out), and at that point a local ruler, Austrian Prince d'Elboef, was informed of the unique items that had been found. Once the magnificent stage with its dedicatory inscriptions had been cleared, the site was named as Herculaneum and the intermittent excavations began. When this city played out, Neapolitan authorities then switched their attention to "La Citta" further down the coast.

There are technical reasons for the irregular excavations. Herculaneum's horizontal cover of hardened volcanic mud, far more pliant than the vertical mixture of ashes and lapilli at Pompeii, covers the city to a depth of 60+ feet but left walls and upper storeys quite intact. All the mud must be removed with mining tools and examined, and the exposed walls must be reinforced. Secondly, the modern town of Ercolano is located directly over a part of the city and has refused to be moved. Thirdly, Pompeii has always been attractive due to its greater size, ease of excavation, and the constancy with which "treasure" is found, although at Herculaneum the Villa of the Papyri, once belonging to L. Calpurnius Piso, Caesar's father-in-law, is the biggest yet found and has produced a whole library of literary papyri and many works of art. Since the days of Fiorelli (1860) scientific excavation has been the rule, whenever work was done.

In view of the current excavations which have brought some of the city into the light of day and in view of the extensive tunneling done by early excavators below Ercolano, we are able to state that Pompeii and Herculaneum shared the same history up to 79: both were victimized by the earthquake of 63 and slain by the eruption of 79 — though at different times. Herculaneum was completely sealed off, and because of the depth none sought to recover property. Hence the massive survival.

Herculaneum's area is about one third of that of Pompeii, and its population was only a fourth of that of Pompeii. It was full of private villas, luxury shops, a few public buildings, and some apartment houses. Its position on a promontory near Naples, though healthful, killed off its commercial potential. Thus it seems to have been a sleepy little provincial town. This is attested by the small quantity of recovered graffiti. The inhabitants of the town seem to have been above this — unfortunately for us. In the surviving texts we can follow the influence of several citizens of the town, while also noting the usual types of "formal" inscriptions. It must be emphasized that the above picture is liable to extensive revision depending on the progress of future discoveries, but the above is a well-reasoned intelligent guess.

A bronze military diploma from Emperor Vespasian:

Imperator Vespasianus Caesar Augustus, tribuniciā potestate, consul II, veteranis, qui militaverunt in Legione II Adiutrice, Pia, Fideli, qui vicena stipendia aut plura meruerant et sunt dismissi honestā missione (quorum nomina subscripta sunt), et ipsis liberis posterisque eorum civitatem dedit et conubium cum   5 uxoribus, quas tunc habuissent cum est civitas iis data aut (siqui caelibes essent) cum iis quas postea duxissent dumtaxat singuli singulas.

Ante diem Nones Martias Imperatore Vespasianō Caesare Augusto II, Caesaris Augusti filiō, consule, Tabulā I, paginā V, locō   10 XXXXVI.

Descriptum et recognitum ex tabulā aeneā. quae fixa est Romae in Capitoliō in podiō Arae Gentis Iuliae latere dextrō ante signum Liberi patris. *(1402)*

On the Temple of Cybele:

Imperator Caesar Vespasianus Augustus, Pontifex Maximus, tribuniciā potestate VII, imperator XVII, pater patriae, consul VII, designatus VIII, templum Matris Deum terrae motū conlapsum restituit. *(1406)*

The Imperial Family:

Divo Iulio Herculanenses. *(1410)*
Divo Iulio Augustales. *(1411, 1412)*
Divae Augustae L. Mammius Maximus pecuniā suā. *(1413)*
Tiberio Caesari, Divi Augusti filio, Divi Iuli nepoti, Augusto, Pontifici Maximo, consuli V, imperatori VIII, tribuniciā potestate XXXIIX, decretō decurionum. *(1414)*
Tiberio Claudio, Drusi filio, Caesari Augusto, Germanico, Pontifici Maximo, tribuniciā potestate VIII, imperatori XVI, consuli IIII, patri patriae, censori, ex testamentō . . . *(1416)*

1402 2/3. notice the lgion's nicknames. 5. civitas: 'citizenship'. 7. duxissent: 'married', to be supplied in next line. 13/4. These items no longer are visible 1406. deum = deorum. designatus: sc. *consul* imperator + number. 'commander-in-chief ——times
1416. Caesari Augusto: trans. with the rest of imperial name at start, then the patronymic. Germanico: another new nichname.

Antoniae Augustae, matri Ti. Claudi Caesaris Augusti Germanici, pontificis maximi, L. Mammius Maximum pecuniā suā. *(1417)*

Iuliae, Germanici filiae, Agrippinae, Tiberis Claudi Caesaris Augusti, Germanici, pontificis maximi, tribuniciā potestate, patris patriae, L. Mammius Maximum pecuniā suā. *(1418)*

Imperatori T. Vespasiano Caesari, Augusti filio, tribuniciā potestate, consuli II, censori, pontifici M. Nonius. *(1420)*

The local greats:

Appius Pulcher, Cai filius, consul, imperator VI, vir epulonum. *(1423)*

Appio Claudio, Cai filio, Pulchro, consuli, imperatori, Herculanenses post mortem. *(1424)*

M. Nonius, Marci filius, Balbus, proconsule, basilicam, portas, murum pecuniā suā. *(1425)*

M. Nonio, Marci filio, Balbo, praetori, proconsule, Herculanenses. *(1426, 1427)*

M. Nonio, Marci filio, Balbo, praetori, proconsule, decretō decurionum *(1428)*

M. Nonio, Marci filio, Balbo, proconsule, Nucherini municipes sui. *(1429)*

M. Nonio, Marci filio, Balbo, proconsule, commune Cretensium patrono. *(1430-32)*

M. Nonio, Marci filio, Balbo, praetori, proconsule, Gortynei, aere collatō. *(1434)*

M. Nonio, Marci filio, Balbo, patri, decretō decurionum. *(1439)*

Volasenniae, Cai filiae, Tertiae Balbi, decuriones Herculanenses. *(1436)*

Volasenniae, Cai filiae, Tertiae Balbi, decuriones et pleps Herculanensis. *(1435)*

Viciriae, Auli filiae, Archadae, matri Balbi, decretō decurionum. *(1440)*

GENERAL NOTE: thruout this section one can supply HOC MONUMENTUM DEDICAVIT or equivalent to make a complete sentence, just as one learns to deal with the patronymics and titles.
1418. Germanicus Caesar takes up most of the text. Germanici: 'victor over Germany 1425ff. This is the renowned Balbus family, statues of which survive in quantity in the entrance gallery of the Musco Nazionale in Naples, one of whom served his country in Crete 1435. pleps - plebs 1436. Menusia: 'of the Menusian (tribe).

L. Annius, Luci filius, Mammianus Rufus, IIvir quinquennalis, theatrum (et) orchestram suā pecuniā. *(1443-45)*

P. Numisius, Publici filius, Menusia, architectus. *(1446)*

M. Calatorio, Marci filio, Quartioni, municipes et incolaẹ, aere conlatō. *(1447)*

L. Mammius Maximus macellum cum ornamentis et meritoris suā pecuniā faciendum curavit idemque dedicatione populo epulum dedit. *(1450)*

L. Mammio Maximo, Augustali, municipes et incolae, aere conlato. *(1452)*

M. Spurius, Marci filius, Meneniā, Rufus, IIVir iure dicundo, macellum de suā pecuniā faciendum curavit idemque probavit.
(1457)

Burial spots:

Decretō decurionum locus sepulturae publice datus (est) L. Ausidio, Luci filio, Hor. . . Montan. . . , comiti C. Calvisi Sabini.
(1468)

M. Monio, Balbi liberto, Eutychio Marciano locum sepulturae decretō decurionum. *(1471)*

Dis Manibus Caerinae Restitutae, T. Flavi Domiti coniugis benemerentis. Vixit annis XXXXIII. *(1477)*

THE THEATRE, RESTORED

1450. faciendum: sc. *esse.* dedicatione: abl. of time when 1477. one of the most common type of funeral texts - the most common kind of Latin text. GENERAL NOTE ON DATES: see Appendix V for conversion to our calendar. par, paris, n. 'pair'. Herculanei: locative case.

THE GRAFFITI OF HERCULANEUM

ANNOUNCEMENTS OF GAMES:

VIII Kalendas Martias Numisii Genialis gladiatorum paria X
Herculanei *(10579)*

CALENDAR DATES

XVII Kalendas, X Kalendas, VII Idus *(10510)*
X Kalendas Februarias *(10617)*
VIII Kalendas Iulias *(10683)*

POLITICAL MATTERS

a. two prayers
   Municipes, iuvate Caesarem. *(10479)*
   Felicitati Caesaris supplicate. *(10487)*
b. a municipal problem
   M. Alficius Paulus, aedilis, velit in hunc locum †stercus† abi-
   cere; movetur; non iacere. *(10488)*

THE ECONOMY

a. a label
   Rufula pondo VS *(10548)*

b. a receipt list with jibberish
   aquaria dua cum basis
   aqua in manus dua cum basis
   hamas duas cum basis
   aqua in manū cotidianā CII
      cum basis
      urciolos duos
   candelabra quatuor et lucubra-
      torium unum
   lucerna aenea
   hamula una

   pelvis cum basim et lytrum
   guttos tres
   scapheola dua
   ferreas strigiles septem
   haenas quattuor
   marmor cum basim
   aenea fuminaria dua
            (10566)

10488. Some strange goings-on in this text: velit=vult   stercus = stercum
abicere = abici. movetur: 'it is to be moved'. non iacere: once again
supply *M. Alficius Paulus, aedilis, velit* 10566. a vast list of items with a
keen disregard of cases and spelling; yet this is how some grafitti appear —
a challenge for all!

58

c. memos

    Vinum acceptum ab domino VII Idus Apriles *(10565)*
    II Idus Septembres pro tunicā denarium I, asses VII *(10664)*
    XI Kalendas panem factum
    III Nonas panem factum *(10575)*
    Qunei XXIII, anseres XV *(10670)*

LITERATURE AND PROVERBS

a. a student unhappy with Ovid
    Ovidio salutem; moriēris Tomis. Feliciter! *(10595)*

b. two adages
    Qui si tutari nescit, nescit vivere.
    Minimum malum fit contemnendō maximum. *(10634)*

GREETINGS AND SALUTATIONS

a. Hurrah!
    Famulus Sereno feliciter! *(10491)*
    Ainiciae feliciter! *(10511)*
    Feliciter Proculo! *(10700)*

b. Leave-takings
    Amandus Surus Ianuari vale! *(10513)*
    Echio, vale! *(10643b)*
    Amethyste, vale! *(10649)*
    Longine, vale! *(10672)*

c. a variation on a theme
    Vivanius Ater ubique! *(10686)*

d. best epistolatory form
    Hyacinthus hīc fuit; Verginiae suae salutem! *(10525)*
    Prigenio salutem! *(10531)*

10565. acceptum: sc. *est* to make a full sentence, as thruout in so much
of Latin! 10575. panem: acc. may be due to an implied indir. statement
10595. Ovidio: sc. *dico* as main verb 10634. qui: 'anyone 10491. Famu-
lus: sc. *dicit* as below, where other names in the nominative case are seen,
10529 & 10531. salutem: sc. *dicit.*

MERE MESSAGES

a. too much of a good thing
   Mansi solus ex senatus consultō *(10501)*
   Ex senatus consultō Herculanei mansi solus. *(10503)*
   Vasileus habitat Puteolis in castris Augusti sub Valeriō.
   (10502)

   Saturninae matri uncus detur. *(10519)*

b. friendly advice.
   Caveas, Timinia, fures! *(10600)*

c. from a latrine
   Apollinaris, medicus Titi Imperatoris, hīc cacavit bene.
   (10619)

d. mere flattery
   Iustus cinaedus. *(10654c)*
   Lasius cinaedus *(10671)*

e. by a dejected gladiator
   Ursi me comedant! *(10656, 10660)*

LOVERS' MESSAGES

a. helpful tips
   Si voles cum Marcello bona, . . . *(10541)*
   Masueta, tene! *(10568)*

b. a hopeful
   Hīc amor sitiet! *(10562)*

c. the agony and the ecstacy
   Centurio Centonem non habet. *(10581)*
   Venimus, venimus huc; cupidi multo magis ire cupimus.
   (10640)

10501 & 10503. ex: 'according to 10502. Puteoli: consult your map for
this town's location 10600. caveas = cave, what type of subj? 10654c &
10671, cinaedus: sc. *est* for completeness 10656 & 10660. comedant:
what mood? 10541. unfortunately the later half is lost 01568. Mansueta:
a personal name in this grafitto with picture 10640. multi magis: unfortunately modifying *ire*.

60

Hermeros Primageniae dominae: veni Puteolos in vicō Ti-
minianō et quaere a Messiō nummulariō Hermerotem Phoebi.

(10676)

d. boasters all

Duo sodales hīc fuerunt, et, cum diu malum ministrum
in omnia haberent nomine Epaphroditum, vix tarde eum foras exigerunt. Consumpserunt persuavissime cum futuēre
HS CVS. *(10675)*

Apelles Mus cum fratre Dextrō: amabiliter futuēre bis
binas. *(10678)*

Longinus IV Idus Iulias accepit vim hilare. Sturnus amator.

(10694)

Portunnus amat Ampliandam; Ianuarias amat Veneriam.
Rogamus, domina Venus, ut nos in mente habeas, quod te modo interrogamus. *(10697)*

10676. Hermeros: the older nominative ending, sc. *salutem dicit.* Phoebi:
sc. *filium* 10675. in omnia: 'in every way'. consumpserunt: sc. *tempus*
as dir. obj. HS CVS: expresses the price paid 10678. binas: 'a pair of girls'
10697. quod: 'as for what'.

THE BREAKABLES OF HERCULANEUM

DATES ON THE BOTTLES

Vitelliō Vipstanō consule. *(10718)*
Imperatore III consule. *(10719)*

BRANDS OF WINE

Choum vetus excellens Herculanei Livi Alcini. *(10722)*
Falernum ab Eudoxō *(10724, 10725)*
Vinum rubrum. *(10728b)*

OTHER PRODUCTS CONTAINED

Acetum *(10732)*
Veio Secundo garum *(10734)*
Garum praecellens A. Lu. . . *(10735)*
Garum scombrorum Ti. Claudi Atimeti *(10736)*
Garum flos *(10737)*
Garum flos per se *(10738)*
Liquamen, flos primum *(10743)*
Liquamen optimum *(10744, 10745)*
Liquamen optimum A. Umbrici Scauri *(10746)*
Muria L. Fabii *(10747)*
Cicer columbinum *(10751)*
Mola M. Cameri *(10754)*
Oleti *(10755)*
Vino *(10866)*

SOME DRAMATIS PERSONAE

Felicis Iulciani Montani *(10744)*
Iuli Crispi *(10778)*
Q. Iunio Secundo *(10780)*
Livio Alcimo *(10785)*
Herculanio L. Oppio Clementi *(10798)*
Caecilio Iucundo *(10768)*

MISCELLANY

Pausanias fecit. *(10867)*

10722. Choum: sc. *vinum* thruout 10768. presumably the renowned
banker of Pompeii, whose house, bust, and tablets were uncovered in
1875.

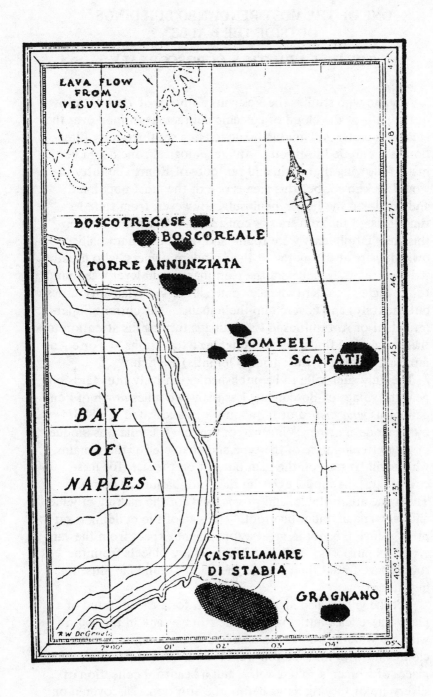

LAVA FLOW
FROM
VESUVIUS

48'

47'

46'

BOSCOTRECASE
BOSCOREALE

TORRE ANNUNZIATA

45'

POMPEII
SCAFATI

44'

BAY
OF
NAPLES

43'

40° 42'

CASTELLAMARE
DI STABIA

GRAGNANO

R.W. DeGroote

2° 00'   01'   02'   03'   04'   05'

ONE OF THE MOST RENOWNED BUILDINGS
OUTSIDE THE WALLS

THE VILLA RUSTICA AT BOSCOREALE

Anyone who studies the Vesuvius eruption of 79 A.D. knows of the path of the cloud of volcanic debris that formed over the volcano's crater and gradually moved in a southwesterly direction as it emptied itself out. An archeological zone could be made following that path, and far more of Roman country life would be known, but this area is one of the most populated and fertile on the Italian peninsula. However, from time to time through the centuries as construction was being done in this area, farmhouses were found and, not being nationally owned, were at the mercy of their modern owners, who usually stripped the walls and sold the paintings or whatever was found to the highest bidder (whence come all the Vesuvian antiquities outside Italy) and covered up the remains. The current Superintendent of Antiquities in Campania is turning his attention to these neglected finds, and the ongoing excavations at Torre Annunziata (probably the ancient Oplontis) are rich.

The only such villa to be published extensively thus far is one near the village of Boscoreale, less than two miles north of Pompeii. This *villa rustica* or farmhouse was excavated in 1893/4 by its modern owner, Vincenzo di Prisco. The villa was unique in the extreme rarity of the type and character of the remains, which will be seen on the plan but not on the site (for it is covered up). A model exists in the Antiquarium at Pompeii. The living areas, stable, and rooms used for the making of wine and oil were all under one roof. The size of the building is surprising since it is not as great as one might expect from the variety of its purposes: 130 by 82 feet. Many objects from the rooms have found their way to the Field Columbian Museum in Chicago.

Yet the villa is also highly significant for a cache found in a place where least anticipated — the storage tank in the room with the wine press. Here a man had taken refuge from the cloud, and with his skeleton were found 1,000 gold coins, many pieces of women's gold jewelry, and a beautiful collection of silverware of varying dates before the eruption. Discovered on

April 6, 1895, by Signor di Prisco, the silverware was brought to Paris and immediately bought by Baron de Rothschild, who presented the 95 pieces to the Louvre. Several pieces that had gotten separated were given to the Louvre at the same time for a total of 102 pieces. The lady's jewelry came to the Louvre in 1896 for a total of 110 pieces.

Of the decorative pieces the finest is the shallow bowl with an allegorical representation of the city of Alexandria, Egypt, in high relief, fully described by Mau. Among the 16 cups a pair, 4 inches high and ornamented with skeletons (some signed as figures in Greek literature, the philosophers Zeno and Epicurus with the dramatists Sophocles and Euripides) in high relief, is so grouped that each cup represents four scenes satirizing human life and its interpretation in poetry and philosophy with accompanying Greek texts, given below separately, which explain either the depicted subject or the philosophic tendency represented. These were made by a Greek for a Pompeiian lady, Gavia. Below are the various texts on the treasure as described and published by A. Heron de Villefosse in 1903. In some instances the name of a later owner has been scratched on the surface with a pointed tool, as we deal with a silver collection of a woman named Maxima, who got her specimens from different sources. Note with care the illustrations of these treasures, the best of the three silver caches thus far preserved from antiquity.

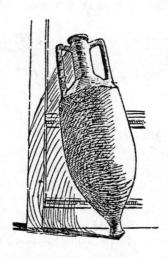

THE TEXTS FROM THE BOSCOREALE TREASURE

The name's the thing:

Maximae (33 times)
Maximae nostrae *(61, 89, 90)*
Priami (et) Maximae   *(5, 85, 86, 87, 88)*
Priami *(6)*
Holconi *(18)*   5
Tubertae *(49)*
L. Caecili Herennae *(84, 85, 86, 87)*

Weights and Measures:

pondo III, scripula VIII   *(19)*
pondo I, uncias III semunciam, scripula II *(24)*   9

From the Alexandrian patera:

phiala et emblema pendentia: pondo II, uncias X, scripula V;
phiala pendens: pondo II, uncias II semunciam emblema pendens: pondo . . , uncias VII semunciam   *(1)*

Combinations:

Gaviae; pondo II, uncias VIII, scripula IIII *(7)*
M. Atti Clari II vasa: pondo IV semissem, scripula VI semun-   15
ciam *(17)*
Pamphili Caesaris liberti IV vasa: pondo III, scripula IV *(27,
28, 29, 30)*
Maximae calices: pondo II semissem *(97)*

Miscellaneous:

M. Domitius Polygnos †fece†   *(21)*

A GENERAL NOTE ON ROMAN WEIGHTS: 24 scripuli ('scruples') = 1
unicia ('ounce'); 12 unciae = 1 pondo ('pound' – an indeclinable word').
#1 This is the text on the lovely Alexandria bowl (phiala) with the
emlema, the stunning head of a goddess in relief. #7ff. These are the renowned cups with the Greek text. 19. fece: misspelling of *fecit.*

A.	*Entrance Court*
B.	*Kitchen*
C-F.	*Bath*
H.	*Stable*
J.	*Tool Room*
K-L.	*Sleeping Rooms*
M.	*Anteroom*
N.	*Dining Room*
O.	*Bakery*
P.	*Room with Two Wine Presses*
Q.	*Corridor*
R.	*Court for the Fermentation of Wine*
S.	*Barn*
T.	*Threshing Floor*
V.	*Sleeping Rooms*
W.	*Cellar Entrance*
X.	*Room with Hand Mill*
Y.	*Room with Oil Press*
Z.	*Room with Olive Crusher*

PLAN OF THE VILLA RUSTICA AT BOSCOREALE

Sentences on the skeleton cups:

    Grasp hold of life, for tomorrow is unsure!
    Life is a stage!
    Enjoy yourself while alive!
    Enjoyment is the ultimate! *(7)*
    Honor filth devoutly!
    That's mankind!
    Be merry as long as you are alive! *(8)*

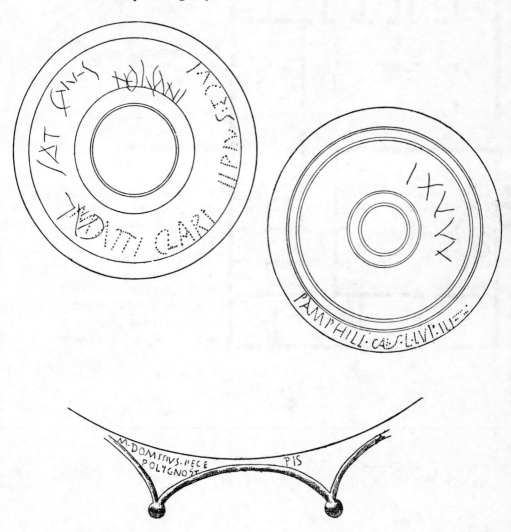

HIGHLIGHTS FROM THE
CENA TRIMALCHIONIS OF PETRONIUS

Arrival at Trimalchio's House

XXVIII. Sequimur nos admiratione iam saturi et cum Agamem-
none ad ianuam pervenimus, in cuius poste libellus erat cum
hāc inscriptione fixus:

QVISQVIS SERVVS SINE DOMINICO IVSSV FORAS
EXIERIT, ACCIPIET PLAGAS CENTVM.

In aditū autem ipsō stabat ostiarius prasinatus, cerasinō suc-   6
cintus cingulō, atque in lance argenteā pisum purgabat. Super
limen autem cavea pendebat aurea, in quā pica varia intrantes
salutabat. XXIX. Ceterum ego dum omnia stupeo, paene
resupinatus crura mea fregi. Ad sinistram enim instrantibus non   10
longe ab ostiarii cellā canis ingens, catenā vinctus, in pariete erat
pictus superque quadratā litterā scriptum:

CAVE CANEM.

Et collegae quidem mei riserunt; ego autem collectō spiritū
non destiti totum parietem persequi. Erat autem venalicium   15
cum titulis pictum, et ipse Trimalchio capillatus caduceum tene-
bat Minervāque ducente Romam intrabat. Hinc quemadmodum
ratiocinari didicisset deinque dispensator factus esset, omnia
diligenter curiosus pictor cum inscriptione reddiderat. In defi-
ciente vero iam porticū levatum mentō in tribunal excelsum   20
Mercurius rapiebat. Praesto erat Fortuna cum cornū abundanti
copiosā et tres Parcae aurea pensa torquentes. Notavi etiam in
porticū gregem cursorum cum magistrō se exercentem. Praeterea grande armarium in angulō vidi, in cuius aediculā erant
Lares argentei positi Venerisque signum marmoreum et pyxis   25

1. admiratione: abl. after *saturi.* 5. exi(v)erit. fut. perf. of *exeo* in a con-
ditional clause. 8. intrantes: sc. *nos.* 9. ceterum = sed. 10. intrantibus: sc.
nobis. 12. scriptum: sc. *erat,* 'there had been written'. 15. persequi: inf.
after *destitui.* 16. caduceum: the wand of Mercury, god of gain. 17/18.
quemadmodum . . . esset: indir. ques. after *reddiderat,* 'showed'. 19/20
In porticu: 'at the end of the columnade.' levatum: sc *Trimalchionem.*
21/22. cornu capiosa: usually written as our cornucopia. 25. Lares:
the Roman household gods.

aurea non pusilla, in quā barbam ipsius conditam esse dicebant.
Interrogare ergo atriensem coepi, quas in mediō picturas haberent.
"*Iliada et Odyssian*" inquit "ac Laenatis gladitorium munus."
Non licebat multas iam picturas considerare.

In the Dining Room

XXX. Nos iam ad triclinium perveneramus, in cuius parte primā   5
procurator rationes accipiebat. Et — quod praecipue miratus sum —
in postibus triclinii fasces erant cum securibus fixi, quorum
imam partem quasi embolum navis aeneum finiebat, in quō erat
scriptum:

C. POMPEIO TRIMALCHIONI, SEVIRO AVGVSTALI,   10
CINNAMVS DISPENSATOR.

Sub eōdem titulō et lucerna bilychnis de camerā pendebat, et
duae tabulae in utrōque poste defixae, quarum altera (si bene
memini) hoc habebat inscriptum:

III ET PRIDIE KALENDAS IANVARIAS C. NOSTER   15
FORAS CENAT.
altera habebat lunae cursum stellarumque, septem imagines pictas;
et qui dies boni quique incommodi essent, distinguente bullā
notabantur.

The First Course and Its Service

XXXI. Allata est gustatio valde lauta; nam iam omnes discubu-   20
erant praeter ipsum Trimalchionem, cui locus novō more primus
servabatur. Ceterum in promulsidari asellus erat Corinthius cum
bisacciō positus, qui habebat olivas in alterā parte albas, in alterā nigras. Tegebant asellum duae lances, in quarum marginibus
nomen TRIMALCHIO inscriptum erat et argenti pondus. Ponti-   25
culi etiam ferruminati sustinebant glires melle ac papavere sparsos

1. ipsius = Trimalchionis. 2. medio: sc. *porticu.* 3. Iliada, Odyssian:
Greek accusative endings. 6. quod: 'what'. 8. quasi: 'like'. 10. seviro
Augustali: 'an Augustal commissioner', a freedman in charge of emper-
or worship. 11. dispensator: sc. *hoc. dedicavit.* 12. et: adv. 'also'.
18. qui . . . essent: indir. ques. after *notabantur.* 21. primus locus:
Trimalchio takes the *summus in summo* rather than *summus in imo.*
25. pondus: sc. *inscriptum erat,* such is seen on the Boscoreale
Treasure.

Fuerunt et tomacula supra craticulam argenteam ferventia posita
et infra craticulam Syrica pruna cum granis Punici mali.

XXXIV. Ceterum inter tumultum cum forte paropsis excidisset
et puer iacentem sustulisset, animadvertit Trimalchio colaphisque
obiurgari puerum ac proicere rursus paropsidem iussit. Insecutus   5
est lecticarius argentumque inter reliqua purgamenta scopis coepit
everrere. Subinde intraverunt duo Aethiopes capillati cum pu-
sillis utribus (quales solent esse qui harenam in ampitheatrō
spargunt) vinumque dedēre in manus; aquam enim nemo porrexit.

The Wine Course with an Incident

Statim allatae sunt amphorae vitreae diligenter gypsatae,   10
quarum in cervicibus pittacia erant affixa cum hōc titulō:

FALERNVM OPIMIANVM ANNORVM CENTVM.

Dum titulos perlegimus, complausit Trimalchio manus et "Eheu"
inquit "ergo diutius vivit vinum quam homuncio. Quare tengo-
menas faciamus! Vita vinum est! Verum Opimianum praesto.   15
Heri non tam bonum posui, et multo honestiores cenabant."
Potantibus ergo nobis et accuratissime lautitias mirantibus lar-
vam argenteam attulit servus sic aptatam ut articuli eius verte-
braeque luxatae in omnem partem flecterentur. Hanc cum super
mensam semel iterumque abiecisset et catenatio mobilis aliquot   20
figuras exprimeret, Trimalchio adiecit:

"Eheu nos miseros, quam totus homuncio nil est!
Sic erimus cuncti, postquam nos aufert Orcus.
Ergo vivamus, dum licet esse bene!"

The Host's Background

XXXVII. "Ipse Trimalchio fundos habet, quā milvi volant, num-   25
morum nummes. Argentum in ostiarii illius cellā plus iacet quam

1. fuerunt posita = posita sunt et: adv. 4. iacentem: sc. *paropsidem*
animadvertit: sc. *id* in: 'for'. 12. Falernum Opimianum: sc. *vinum*
as with *bonum*. 15. Opimainum: sc. *vinum est.* 22. nos miseros: acc.
of exclamation quam: 'now'. 25/6. nummorum nummos: 'heaps
and heaps', argentum plus 'more more'.

quisquam in fortunis habet.   Familiā vero non mehercules puto
decumam partem esse quae dominum suum noverit. Ad summum,
quemvis es istis babaecalis in rutae folium coniciet.   XXXVIIII.
Nec est quod putes illum quicquam emere. Omnia domi nascun-
tur: lana, credrae, piper; lacte gallinaceum si quaesiveris, invenies.   5
Ad summum, parum illi bona lana nascebatur; arietes a Tarentō
emit et eos culavit in gregem. Mel Atticum ut domi nasceretur,
apes ab Athenis iussit afferri; obiter et vernaculae quae sunt,
meliusculae a Graeculis fient. Ecce! intra hos dies scripsit ut illi
ex Indiā semen boletorum mitteretur. Nam mulam quidem nullam   10
habet, quae non ex onagrō nata sit. Vides tot culcitras: nulla non
aut conchyliatum aut coccineum tomentum habet. Tanta est
animi beatitudo."

A Report of the Day's Happenings on Estates

LIII. Et plane interpellavit saltationis libidinem actuarius, qui
tamquam *Urbis Acta* recitavit: "VII Kalendas Sextiles: in   15
praediō Cumanō, quod est Trimalchionis, nati sunt pueri XXX,
puellae XL; sublata in horreum ex areā tritici milia modior-
um quingenta; boves domiti quingenti. Eōdem diē: Mithradates
servus in crucem actus est, quia Gai nostri genio maledixerat.
Eōdem diē: in arcam relatum est, quod collocari non potuit,   20
sestertium centies. Eōdem diē: incendium factum est in hortis
Pompeianis, ortum ex aedibus Nastae vilici." "Quid?" inquit
Trimalchio "quando mihi Pompeiani horti empti sunt?" "Anno
priore" inquit actuarius "et ideo in rationem nondum venerunt."
Excanduit Trimalchio et "Quicumque" inquit "mihi fundi empti   25
fuerint, nisi intra sextum mensem sciero, in rationes meas inferri
vetuo."

3. quemvis: 'anyone' in . . .folium: 'into a cocked hat'. 4. quicquam:
subj. of *est:* there is not a thing', domi: locative. 5. lacte gallinaceum:
our 'hen's teeth'. 6. illi: 'for him'. 7. Mel Atticum: one of the finest
honeys of the ancient world. 8. obiter = simul et: adv. 9. fient:sc.
apes as subj. and antecedent of *quae*. 15. Urbis = Romae. 21. sestertium centies: HS 1,000,000 25. quicumque: with *fundi.* 13. sciero =
scivero.

The Incident of the Lares

IX. Inter haec tres pueri, candidas succincti tunicas, intraverunt, quorum duo Lares bullatos super mensam posuerunt. Unus, pateram vini circumferens, "Dei propitii!" clamabat. Trimalchio ait unum Cerdonem, alterum Felicionem, tertium Lucrionem vocari. Nos etiam veram imaginem ipsius Trimalchionis, cum iam   5
omnes basiaverunt, erubuimus praeterire.

The Entry of the Sevir Habinnas

LXV. Inter haec triclinii valvas lictor percussit. Amictus veste albā, cum ingenti frequentiā comissator intravit. Ego, maiestate conterritus, praetorem putabam venisse. Itaque temptavi assur-gere et nudos pedes in terram deferre. Risit hanc trepidationem   10
Agamemnon et "Contine te" inquit "homo stultissime! Habinnas sevir est idemque lapidarius, qui videtur monumenta optime facere."

LXXI. Respiciens deinde Habinnam, "Quid dicis" inquit "amice carissime? Aedificas monumentum meum, quemadmodum te   15
iussi? Valde te rogo, ut secundum pedes statuae meae catellam ponas et coronas et unguenta et Petraitis omnes pugnas ut mihi contiguat tuō beneficiō post morten vivere; praeterea ut sint in fronte pedes centum, in agrum pedes ducenti. Omne genus enim poma volo sint circa cineres meos et vinearum largiter. Valde   20
enim falsum est vivo quidem domos cultas esse, non curari eas, ubi diutius nobis habitandum est. Et ideo ante omnia adici volo:

HOC MONVMENTVM HEREDEM NON SEQVITVR.

Ceterum erit mihi curae ut testamentō caveam, ne mortuus iniuriam accipiam. Praeponam enim unum ex libertis sepulchrō   25
meō custodiae causā, ne in monumentum meum populus cacatum

1. tunicas: Greek accusative. 3. dei: sc. *sint*. 4. The divinities' names mean respectively Business, Luck, and Gain. 12. idemque: 'and also'.. 16. secundum: a preposition. 17. Petraitis: 'of P.', a noted gladiator even seen in Pomeian grafitti. 17/18. ut . . .vivere: 'so that I can live'. 20. Vinearum largiter: 'lots of vines', parallel with *poma*. 21. falsum: 'silly' vivo: 'of a living man' eas: sc. *domos*. 22. nobis . . .est: 'where we must live'. 24. certerum . . .curae = sed curabo mortuus: 'while dead'. 26. cacatum: the rarely seen supine.

currat. Te rogo ut naves etiam in lateribus monumenti mei facias
plenis velis euntes et me in tribunali sedentem praetextatum cum
anulis aureis quinque et nummos in publicō de sacculō effunden-
tem. Scis enim, quod epulum dedi binos denarios. Faciantur,
si tibi videtur, et triclinia. Facias et totum populum sibi suaviter   5
facientem. Ad dexteram meam ponas statuam Fortunatae meae
columbam tenentem: et catellam cingulō alligatam ducat; et
cicaronem meum et amphoras copiosas gypsatas, ne effluant
vinum. Et urnam licet fractam sculpas et super eam puerum
plorantem et Horologium in mediō, ut quisquis horas inspiciet,   10
et (velit nolit) nomen meum legat. Inscriptio quoque vide diligenter si haec satis idonea tibi videtur:

C. POMPEIVS TRIMALCHIO MAECENATIANVS HIC
REQVIESCIT.
HVIC SEVIRATVS ABSENTI DECRETVS EST.   15
CVM POSSET IN OMNIBVS DECVRIIS ROMAE ESSE, TAMEN
NOLVIT.
PIVS, FORTIS, FIDELIS, EX PARVO CREVIT.
SESTERTIVM RELIQVIT TRECENTIES
NEC VMQVAM PHILOSOPHVM AVDIVIT.   20
VALE: ET TV.

The Source of Trimalchio's Money

LXXVI. Dominus coheredem me Caesari fecit et accept patrimonium laticlavium. Nemini tamen nihil satis est. Concupivi
negotiari. Ne multis vos morer, quinque naves aedificavi, oneravi
vinum − et tunc erat contra aurum − misi Romam. Putares me   25
hoc iussisse: omnes naves naufraga runt; factum sed fabula!
Unō diē Neptunus trecenties sestertium devoravit. Putares me
defecisse? Non mehercules mi haec iactura gusti fuit, tamquam

---

2. euntes: part. from *eo* with *naves.* 4. epulum: appos. with *denar-*
ius. 5. videatur: 'it seems best'. et: adv. sibi . . .facientem: 'doing
nicely by itself'. 8. cicaronem: sc. *facias.* 9. licet sculpas: 'may
you portray'. 11. velit nolit: 'willynilly' inscriptio: with *haec.*
24. multis: sc. *verbis.* 25. contra aurum: 'as good as gold' misi: sc.
aurum as dir. obj. 28. gusti: gen of value 'worth a . . .'

nihil facti. Alteras feci maiores et meliores et feliciores, ut nemo
non me virum fortem diceret. Scitis, magna navis magnam forti-
tudinem nabet. Oneravi rursus vinum, lardum, fabam, seplasium,
mancipia. Hōc locō Fortunata rem piam fecit; omne enim aurum
suum et omnia vestimenta vendidit et mi centum aureos in manū   5
posuit. Hoc fuit peculii mei fermentum. Cito fit quod dei volunt.
Unō cursū centies sestertium corrotundavi. Statim redemi fundos omnes, qui patroni mei fuerant. Aedifico domum. Ut
scitis, casula erat; nunc templum est. Habet quattuor cenationes,
cubicula viginti, porticus marmeratos duos, susum cenationem,   10
cubiculum in quō ipse dormio, viperae huius sessorium, ostarii
cellam perbonam; hospitium hospites capit.''

The Dinner's End

   Ibat res ad summam nauseam, cum Trimalchio, ebrietate tur-
pissimā gravis, novum acroama, cornicines, in triclinium iussit
adduci. Fultus cervicalibus multis extendit se super torum ex-   15
tremum et "Fingite me" inquit "mortuum esse. Dicite aliquid
belli.'' Consonuēre cornicines funebri strepitū. Unus praecipue
servus libitinarii illius, qui inter hos honestissimus erat, tam
valde intonuit ut totam concitaret viciniam. Itaque vigiles, qui
custodiebant vicinam regionem, rati ardere Trimalchionis domum,   20
effregerunt ianuam subito et cum aquā securibusque tumultuari
suo iure coeperunt. Nos, occasionem opportunissimam nacti,
Agamemnoni verba dedimus raptimque tam plane quam ex
incendiō fugimus.

                                                                      25

BEWARE OF THE DOG !

AN ANCIENT GALLEY (FROM A POMPEIAN FRESCO).

1. facti = factum est alteras: sc. *naves*. 6. quod. sc. *id* is subj. and
antecedent. 8. patroni mei: genitive. 11. viperae: T's wife. 13. res
'the situation'. 15. torum extremem: 'the end of couch'. 16. aliquid
belli: 'something nice', part. gen. 20. rati: from *reor* = putantes. 22.
nacti = capientes 23. verba dedimus: 'excused ourselves'. tam . . .
quam: 'just as if'.

APPENDIX I

THE OTHER REFERENCES TO THE DISASTER

SENECA THE YOUNGER ON THE EARTHQUAKE

Lucius Annaeus Seneca was born at Corduba, Spain, in 4 B.C.
His influential father had him educated in Rome. Seneca the
Younger, as he is more commonly called, followed the *cursus
honorum*. He aroused the wrath of the Emperor Caligula and
was almost slain. Banished to Corsica in 41 A.D., he remained
there for eight years until summoned to be the tutor to the
future emperor Nero. His control over Nero in the early years
of the reign made the Empire thrive, but as Nero grew worse, he
ordered his old tutor to take his own life. This he did in quiet
dignity. His extant works include twelve moral *Dialogi* and
several parlor tragedies on Greek subjects. Most famous is the
Apocolocyntosis (Pumpkinification) of the Emperor Claudius
and his *Naturales Quaesitiones,* an examination of natural phenomena from the Stoic point of view. From the last-mentioned
work comes the following account.

We have just had news, my esteemed Lucilius, that Pompeii,
the celebrated city in Campania, has been overwhelmed in an
earthquake, which shook all the surrounding districts as well.
The city, you know, lies on a beautiful bay, running far back from
the open sea, and is surrounded by two converging shores: on the
one side that of Surrentum and Stabiae, on the other that of Herculaneum. The disaster happened in winter, a period in which
our forefathers used to claim immunity from such dangers. On
the 5th of February, in the consulship of Regulus and Virginius,
this shock occurred, involving widespread destruction over the
whole province of Campania; this district had never been without
risk of such a calamity but had hitherto been exempt from it, having escaped time after time from groundless alarm.

The extent of the disaster may be gathered from a few details.
Part of the town of Herculaneum fell; the buildings left standing
are very insecure. The colony of Nuceria had painful experience of
the shock but sustained no damage. Naples was just touched by
what might have proved a great disaster to it; many private houses

76

suffered, but no public building was destroyed. The villas built on
the cliffs everywhere shook but without damage being done. In
addition, they say, a flock of 600 sheep was destroyed, and statues
were split open; some people were driven out of their minds and
wandered about in helpless idiocy.

Naturales Quaesitiones VI, 1, trans. Clarke

The effect of the quake of 63 A.D. in the Forum of Pompeii
is preserved on two bas-reliefs at the shrine of the Lares in the
home of L. Caecilius Jucundus, a banker who lived on the Via
di Stabiae in Pompeii (see pp. 00 - 00). The reliefs are no mas-
terpieces, but they do constitute a photographic, almost cine-
matographic document of what the man saw with his own eyes.
The first depicts the north part of the Forum as temples and
arches tumble down, while the second shows what happened at
the Porte Vesuvio at the end of Jucundus' street. All is so exact
that a news photographer, arriving with his camera on the scene,
could not have rendered it more accurately.

MARTIAL'S EPILOGUE ON THE DESTRUCTION OF POMPEII AND HERCULANEUM

The pure literary epigram did not find a home until the days
of Marcus Valerius Martialis, who wrote exclusively in this genre.
Martial did for the epigram what his contemporary, Decimus
Iunius Iuvenalis, did for the satire, viz., they took the loose
strands of the characteristics of the genre that were lying about
and welded them together into one identifiable unit which we
recognize as the epigram and satire, respectively. Born in 40 A.D.
and educated at Bibilis, Spain, Martial went to Rome in 64, lived
there for 34 years, but returned there to Spain in 98, dying about
104. He knew all the important men in Rome, from whom we
hear more than what Martial himself says about his own life.
Showing the great versatility of the genre, he wrote his *Liber
Spectaculorum* for the dedication of the Flavian Amphitheater
(popularly known as the Colosseum) in 79 and thereafter at intervals published the twelve books of the *Liber Epigrammaton*.
Here is a man who could write on anything — something like a
free-lance journalist or a good cartoonist today. If antiquity had

had our newspapers, Martial would not have had to rely on flattery to the cruel Emperor Domitian to buy his bread. He was a victim of his times.

Hic est pampineis viridis modo Vesbius umbris;
  Presserat hic madidos nobilis uva lacus;
Haec auga quam Nysae colles plus Bacchus amavit;
  Hoc nuper Satyri monte dedere choros;
Haec Veneris sedes, Lacedaemone gratior illi;
  Hic locus Herculeo aumine clarus erat.
Cuncta iacent flammis et tristi mersa favilla:
  Nec superi vellent hoc licuiese sibi.

Vesuvius here was green with mantling vine,
  here brimming vats o'erflowed with noble wine.
These hills to jocund Bacchus were more dear
  than Nysam and the Satyrs revelled here.
This blest retreat could Cytherea please,
  this owned the fame of godlike Hercules;
Now dismal ashes all and scorching flame.
  Such dire caprice might move a god to shame.
                    Epigrams IV. 44 (trans. Tatum & Francis)

DIO CASSIUS ON THE ERUPTION OF VESUVIUS

The only other account of any length from antiquity concerning the activity of Mt. Vesuvius in August, 79 A.D. besides Pliny's accounts is the Greek historian Dio Cassius's abridgement of his source, Xiphilenus, that may be found in his *History of Rome* (LXVI. 21-23). Dio was born in Nicea, Asia Minor, became a consul at Rome, and governed Africa and Dalmatia. He found the time to write a Roman history (in Greek) in 80 books, of which 26 survive. It went *ab urbe condita* to 229 A.D. Dio spent 22 years preparing the work. He was a diligent student of earlier history but does not appear to have carried out independent research. His account of the eruption, written about 150 years after the event, still accented the psychological impact.

78

21.   In Campania remarkable and frightful occurrences took place.
For a great fire suddenly flared up at the very end of the summer. It
happened on this wise: Mt. Vesuvius stands over against Naples near
the sea, and it has inexhaustible fountains of fire. Once it was
equally high at all points, and the fire rose from the centre of it; for
here only have the fires broken out, whereas all the outer parts of
the mountain remain even now untouched by fire. Consequently,
as the outside is never burned, while the central part is constantly
growing brittle and being reduced to ashes, the peaks surrounding
the center retain their original height to this day, but the whole section that is on fire, having been consumed, has in the course of time
settled and therefore become concave. Thus the entire mountain re-
sembles an amphitheatre, if we compare great things to small. Its
outlying heights support both trees and vines in abundance, but the
crater is given over to the fire and sends up smoke by day and a
flame by night; in fact, it gives the impression that quantities of in-
cense of all kinds are being burnt in it. This, now, goes on all the
time, sometimes to a greater, sometimes to a lesser extent; but often
the mountain throws up ashes, whenever there is an extensive settling
in the interior and discharges stones whenever it is rent by a violent
blast of air. It also rumbles and roars because its vents are not all
grouped together but are narrow and concealed.

22.   Such is Vesuvius, and these phenomena usually occur there
every year. But all the other occurrences that had taken place in the
course of time, however notable, because unusual, they may have seemed
to those who on each occasion observed them, nevertheless would be regarded as trivial in comparison with what now happened, even if all
had been combined into one. This is what befell.

Numbers of huge men quite surpassing any human stature — such
creatures, in fact, as the Giants are pictured to have been — appeared,
now on the mountains, now in the surrounding country and again
in the cities, wandering over the earth day and night and also flitting
through the air. After this fearful droughts and sudden and violent
earthquakes occurred, so that the whole plain round about seethed
and the summits leaped into the air. There were frequent rumblings,
some of them subterranean, that resembled thunder, and some on the
surface, that sounded like bellowings; the sea also joined in the roar
and the sky re-echoed it. Then suddenly a portentous crash was heard,
as if the mountains were tumbling in ruins; and the first huge stones
were hurled aloft, rising as high as the very summits. Then came a great
quantity of fire and endless smoke, so that the whole atmosphere was
obscured and the sun was entirely hidden, as if eclipsed.

23.   Thus day was turned to night and light into darkness. Some

thought that the Giants were rising again in revolt (for at this time also many of their forms could be discerned in the smoke and, moreover, a sound of trumpets was heard), while others believed that the whole universe was being resolved into chaos or fire. Therefore they fled, some from the houses into the streets, others from outside into houses, now from the sea to the land and now from the land to the sea; for in their excitement they regarded any place where they were not as safer than where they were. While this was going on, an inconceivable quantity of ashes was blown out, which covered both sea and land and filled all the air. It wrought much injury of various kinds, as chance befell, to men and cattle and farms, and in particular it destroyed all fish and birds. Furthermore, it buried two entire cities, Herculaneum and Pompeii, the latter place while its populace was seated in the theatre.

Indeed, the amount of dust, taken all together, was so great that some of it reached Africa and Syria and Egypt, and it also reached Rome, filling the air overhead and darkening the sun. There, too, no little fear was occasioned, that lasted for several days, since the people did not know and could not imagine what had happened, but, like those close at hand, believed that the whole world was being turned upside down, that the sun was disappearing into the earth and that the earth was being lifted to the sky. These ashes, too, did the Romans no great harm at the time, though later they brought a terrible pestilence upon them.

24.   The Emperor Titus sent two ex-consuls to the Campanians to supervise the restoration of the region and bestowed upon the inhabitants not only general gifts of money but also the property of such as had lost their lives and left no heirs. As for himself, he took nothing from any private citizen or city or king, although many kept offering and promising him large sums; but he restored all the damaged regions from funds already on hand.

History of Rome, LXVI, 21-24, trans. Cary

APPENDIX II

AN EARLY REPORT ON THE RENOWNED
PLASTER CORPSES OR CALCHI OF POMPEII

I was anxious to bring back a particular report of some interesting discoveries of human remains lately made at Pompeii. Through the kindness of Signor Vertumni I obtained an introduction to the Cavaliere Fiorelli, the government director of the works, who invited me to join a party shortly about to explore the ruins of Pompeii.

After visiting several of the streets and of the less recently discovered portions of the city, we proceeded to a small museum fitted up under the direction of Signor Fiorelli and in which he hopes to retain, as far as possible, on the spot the numerous objects of interest daily brought to light in the course of the more extended researches which have been made since the advent of the present government of Italy. In two of the rooms in the museum are deposited the bodies, as nearly as possible in the relative positions in which they were found.

It seems that early in February last the remains of a linen cloth or bag were found in the course of removing the loose soil which now covers the remains of Pompeii, that contained several coins, ornaments, and two iron keys. Close to this a hole was accidentally made by one of the workmen with his pickaxe, and, on investigating this, Signor Fiorelli perceived that there existed a cavity of some extent. He had for some time entertained the idea that there were probably human bodies buried in the ruins of the city, the remains of which might have perished though leaving their impressions in the sandy covering. He therefore caused plaster of Paris in a very liquid state to be poured into the cavity; this he continued to do, blowing also with considerable force, so as to cause the liquid plaster to permeate the center cavity.

As soon as the cavity was filled with plaster, he had the earth round it carefully removed. The ashes in which the bodies were buried must have fallen in a damp state and hardened gradually by the lapse of time, and, as the soft parts of the bodies decayed and shrank, a hollow was formed between the bodies and the crust of soil. This formed the cavity into which the plaster was poured. In the bony parts, the space left void being very small, the coat of plaster is proportionately thin and many portions of these extremities and the crania are left exposed. So intimately did these ashes penetrate and so thoroughly has the cast been taken that the texture of the undergarments, drawers, and sort of inner vest with sleeves is distinctly visible.

In the first room is the figure of a female, apparently about 30 years old (or perhaps more), lying on the right side in a twisted and apparently somewhat contorted position. The left hand is raised, and on the little finger is a ring much corroded, apparently of silver; the head is thrown back, and the hair, which appears to have been very plentiful, is still visible; the folds of the dress are quite distinct; the bones of the feet, which are stretched out, are protruding; the ankles and wrist joints and the extremities of the fingers are most delicately formed, and their slenderness and the great length and better proportions of the thumbs would seem to show that this female was of gentler blood than the two hereafter described.

In the next room there is the figure of a man lying on his back with one hand grasping his garment, which he has pulled up to the chest, leaving the whole of the lower portion of the figure exposed, which is of very fine proportions. The other hand is extended and strongly clenched, and the limbs in an attitude of rigidity almost amounting to convulsion.

In the second room also lie two female figures. Signor Fiorelli supposes, probably of the family of the man. They are the bodies of a woman apparently from 30 to 40 and a girl of 15 or 16. The woman is lying on the left side with one arm slightly raised and the other by her side, apparently in an easier position than the two figures before described as if she had suffered less.

The younger is also lying on her left side, the head thus turned in a contrary direction to that of the elder; the face is supported on the left arm, which is placed so as to protect the eyes, and the arm and hand are in an attitude as if holding a cloth or handkerchief over the mouth, apparently protecting herself as much as possible from the falling ashes. The form of this figure is most beautiful; the hand and arm are also very delicate, though both these figures would appear to have been of inferior rank to the first. The tissue of the dress is distinctly visible. I should have mentioned that, in the elder, traces of cloth leglets and the fastenings of a kind of ankle boots are distinctly visible.

The symmetry of the back and loins of this figure, as well as that of the younger already alluded to, are most remarkable, and would seem to go a long way to show that the ancients had actually before them individual specimens of that perfect symmetry which they have handed down to us in those magnificent statues which are still the world's wonder and that they are not an assemblage of the characteristics of different individuals into one imaginary form.

These discoveries are in many particulars worthy of the attention of archeologists and reflect much credit on Signor Fiorelli, to whose acumen they are due.

Augustus Goldschmidt in *Proceedings
of the Society of Antiquaries in
London,* 1863

APPENDIX III

VESUVIUS' UNIQUE LITERARY BURIAL

This was the first ancient library to be discovered; no one dreamed that the sands of Egypt might also contain original ancient manuscripts. It was not until the third year after the discovery of the Villa of the Papyri that a tunnel reached a small room with an elegant marble floor — clearly a study.

THE HOUSE OF THE PAPYRI, RESTORED

Close by was another small room; but this had wooden shelves (carbonized) stacked with what appeared to be cylindrical briquettes stacked on both sides. The briquettes, when examined, proved to be rolls of papyrus badly scorched by the hot mud. But despite the illegibility of the manuscripts, the find excited the world; how fortunate that the villa's owner had preserved his books on papyrus, not paper. A count showed a total of 1787 volumes. The problem was to unroll and read.

In the 18th century no scientific techniques existed to aid in such a task. King Charles of Naples called in a painter, whose diligent efforts resulted in a few works deciphered and many rolls damaged. The attempt was abandoned. Later, Father Antonio Piaggio, a specialist in old manuscripts, was brought from the Vatican Library, and a new effort was begun. A machine was devised to unroll the papyrus; it resembled a contrivance used in wigmaking and unrolled a scroll at the rate of one centimeter an hour. After four years of trial and error and the destruction of many rolls the machine produced results. Three scrolls were unwound, and scholars read a fragment of the *Treatise on Music* by the Greek Epicurean philosopher, Philodemos.

Slowly new scrolls were examined. Piaggio himself worked on them for 40 years. By 1806 some 96 had been deciphered. So eagerly was the world waiting for great new discoveries of the lost literature of antiquity that outsiders like King George IV of England engaged scholars to come to Italy and lend a hand. In the mid-19th century such diverse personages as Pope Pius IX and Czar Nicolas I of Russia came to Naples to see the papyri. At length the general character of the library became clear; and today only 800 scrolls remain unread in the Biblioteca Nazionale in Naples, others being in Oxford. Two unrolled texts are nicely displayed at the Museo Nazionale in Naples.

The fragile papyri included an almost complete collection of the works of Philodemos as well as some works of Epicurus and others. Most of the papyri were in Greek. Of the few in Latin one in particular was beautifully transcribed (see drawing). It was a fragment of an epic poem on the war between Octavianus Caesar and Mark Antony, too broken for inclusion here but at least worthy of mention. It had been written in the same period as Vergil's *Aeneid,* but the author's name was lost. (Subsequently this scroll was presented to Napoleon Bonaparte.) But the anticipated unknown plays, poems, and writing on philosophy, history, and music by the classic masters were missing. The ensuing disappointment was profound. How could so cultivated a person as the owner of this stupendous Villa have collected so specialized a library? Who other than a patron would stock his shelves mainly with the works of a single author, neglecting the many brilliant authors of his own and earlier times?

After J. J. Deiss, *Herculaneum*

APPENDIX IV

THE INITIAL REPORTS ON THE JUCUNDUS FINDS

In 1875/6 a house was excavated on the northern side of
Pompeii. Many houses had been excavated before, but this one
turned out to be truly unique. For a citizen of Pompeii emerged
in all his fullness with enough evidence to place him on book-
shelves with other Roman writers, even if literature was not involved. It was this special find that caused the eminent German
expert on Pompeii, August Mau, to report on the discovery of
the tablets of L. Caecilius Jucundus first and on the house and
its furnishings a year later. Mau's accounts have been translated
from the 1875 and 1876 issues of *Bullettino dell' Instituto di
Corrispondenza Archeologica.* Mau wrote his report in the form
of a letter - not unlike Pliny! To avoid confusion in the student's
mind it should be stated that in his initial report Mau counted
the tablet pages in reverse order from the numeration that he
and the CIL editor of the tablets adopted.

❖❖❖❖❖

You ask me for news of the recent discovery of a collection
of inscribed tablets at Pompeii. What I can tell you I owe to
the kindness of those in charge of the excavations at Pompeii
and to the kindness of Professor di Petra, the director of the
National Museum at Naples, for what concerns the circumstan-
ces of the discovery.

During the excavation of a beautiful house on the eastern
side of Block I of Region V (whose main entrance is the seventh,
counting from the intersection) a square wooden chest was
found in the northern portico of the peristyle at the height of
the architrave between the first and second columns counting
from the east, to be exact. It was about 0.7 meters in each direction and was evidently kept in an upstairs room situated over
that portico. The chest was completely carbonized and disinte-
grated immediately. The tablets contained in it, stacked carefully one on top of the other, were however well preserved,
though they were carbonized. They are all of wood, about 120
millimeters by 90 millimeters in size, and are constructed so as
to form triptychs in the following manner:

Page I, meant to be the cover, is smooth without a layer of
wax. Page II (the back of the first leaf) is waxed and therefore
is protected along the four edges by a raised rim. Page III (the
front of the second leaf) is divided lenghwise into two columns

by means of a depression 2 millimeters deep and 20 millimeters wide. These two columns are almost never waxed, and so the page has no rim. The few times that they are covered with wax however, they are never without the raised rim along the edge, which is broken at top and bottom by the aforesaid depression. Pages IV and V are like Page II, waxed and rimmed. Page VI (the last) served as a cover like Page I and is smooth and without writing. Each triptych has at one edge two holes through which went two strings which formed hinges when tied at the back of the book. In addition to this device, which corresponds to the binding of a modern book, another string tied around the cover kept the three leaves frimly together.

The waxed pages are unfortunately very seldom legible because the thin layer of wax has often been absorbed by the wood, and so the writing has disappeared. Page III on the other hand is almost always written in ink so that the letters are perfectly legible. As to the content, it seems that all of these books are loan contracts and receipts for payment. The contract is written on Pages IV and V, then on Page III go the names of the witnesses (five, seven, or nine in number). Ordinarily, these names are written in the right-hand column so that the left-hand one remained blank, but sometimes the *praenomen* and *nomen* are in the left-hand column and the *cognomen* in the right-hand column. These are not true signatures, since the writing is the same in all; the true signatures are the seals. I find quite plausible the conjecture of Professor di Petra, who believes that the depression on Page III was meant for the seals, since there always remains there a quantity of wax which has spread and spotted the page of witnesses and the opposite page. In the same depression there are traces of threads imbedded in the wax of the seals which points to a special sealing of these last two leaves of the trityth - not to be confused with the outer binding which included all three leaves. On Page II (the back of the first leaf) can also be found a contract which in its wording is not a copy of the one contained on Pages IV and V but is identical in substance.

Thus Professor di Petra finds a general parallel between the arrangement of the Pompeian triptychs and that of military commissions (*diplomata*): there are in both two copies of the document, one of which was sealed. The contract was therefore complete on the final two leaves, but, since it remained sealed, an extract was put on the back of the first leaf that was simply tied to the other two and not sealed. The indication of date is given on some triptyches not only by the names of the consuls but also by the current pair of *duumvirs* (mayors) at Pompeii. The years mentioned so far are 54, 56, 57, and 58 A.D.

This is all that can be said at the present state of things. The tablets, which have been transported with all possible precaution to the National Museum at Naples, are being put in order and recorded in the documents section. When the work is sufficiently advanced, the administration will make it possible for the scientific community to judge the importance of this latest gift of buried Pompeii.

The passageway situated between two shops leads into a spacious Tuscan-style *atrium*, which can also be reached from the shops. It has a pavement of black mosaic with a white stripe along the walls and is ornamented with geometric figures around the plaster-faced *impluvium*. The atrium is symmetrical and has on each side two rooms and a wing. The *peristylum* can be reached from the *tablinum* and from a passageway to the left of this. Through a door at the rear of the left wing one enters the humbler parts of the house, which has a separate entrance and which was probably a separate house originally.

In the front left corner of the atrium stood the Lares' shrine *(lararium)*. Its base, faced with grey marble, has been preserved. It was to carry a tabernacle supported by three small wooden pillars, whose positions can still be clearly seen on the southeast corner and next to the two walls. The walls above the base are white to the height of 1.15 meters, since these sections were hidden behind the tabernacle (which however could hardly have reached this height). At the base two marble steps ran along the two walls, leaving between them and the edge space (0.25 meters) for the pillars. Along the upper edge of the two facades stretches a strip (0.13 meters) with bas-reliefs of an unusual type.

On the south facade, starting from the left, we first see a triumphal arch, then a tetrastyle (four-column) temple shown at an angle such that the left side is the lower. It seems it was intended thus to indicate that the temple is shown head-on but a little from the right. On each side of this temple is seen head-on a man mounted on a mule, placed on a pedestal, stretching his right hand out to the right. The one on the right holds some unidentified object. His legs are spread to an excessive degree, and it seems certain that a caricature was intended here. Before the temple stands a base surmounted by a lit alter. The similarity of such structures of those on the north side of the Forum of of Pompeii is evident. To the right there follows a one-handled vessel set on a bowl with handles; then another altar on which a pig is represented in relief. After this a female bust covered by a kind of canopy supported on each side by a torch. On the right a man approaches, leading a bull while holding an axe in his right hand. Three objects arranged vertically close the strip on this end. These would be instruments for the sacrifice: one object which I cannot identify (two trapezoids joined by arched bands), a knife, and a vessel with a handle above the mouth and three feet in the shape of balls. The strip on the eastern side is divided into small squares by raised lines meeting at right angles. Each of these shows some small object: lizards, insects, vessels of different shapes, various utensils, and other things.

From the wax tablets which were found here we know the name of the owner of this large and important house, whose entrance is the seventh on the east side of the block, counting from the south. The name is also referred to in two painted inscriptions and to which may be added a third on the opposite side of the street (region VI, block 14, between entrances #20 and #21). The same recurs on a small amphora found in the shop at the right of the house's entrance. Even the portrait of L. Caecilius Iucundus has probably come down to us in a herm in the atrium. The head of this herm, which represents a man already old, is of bronze. The marble trunk bears the inscription:
GENIO · L · NOSTRI · FELIX · L.

APPENDIX V

ROMAN ANTIQUITIES

I. Money

2 asses = 1 sestertius or nummus = $ .06
4 sestertii = 1 denarius = $.24
This is the penny or pence of the New Testament.
The denarius, which was worth 17 cents up to the reign of
Augustus, went up to 20 cents until reduced by Nero. It
was the daily wage of a laborer or common soldier.
25 denarii = 1 aureus = $6
The sesterce is represented by the symbol for 2½, properly
IIS (semis), usually represented by the symbol HS.
Nota bene: Please realize that these equivalents in modern
money are at best vague and constantly fluctuate. Yet they
do give one some idea of the ancient sum in modern terms.

II. Measure

16 digiti = 12 unciae = 1 pes = 11.65"
2 pedes = 1 gradus = 2' 5½"
5 pedes = 2 gradus = 1 passus = 4' 10¼ "
125 passus = 1 stadium
8 stadia = mille passus = 4854'

III. The Calendar

Three days of the month have special names from which dates
were reckoned *backward:*
Kalendas, -arum, f., the Kalends, the 1st
Nonae, -arum, f., the Nones, the 7th of March, May, July,
and October, but the 5th of all other months
Idus, -ium, f., the 15th of the same four months, but the
24th of the others

"In March, July, October, and May
the Nones are on the 7th day."

If the date is one of these days, it is expressed in the ablative
with the adjective of the month in agreement. The day immedi-

ately before any of these three is expressed by *pridie* (on the day before) plus the accusative.

Idibus Ianuariis January 1st, *pridie Idus Februarias* Feb 12.

All other dates are expressed as so many days before the next Kalends, Nones, or Ides, whatever is nearest. In reckoning the interval both the date and the Kalends, None, or Ide is included. The expression is all in the accusative, beginning with the words *ante diem,* usually abbreviated to a. d.

March 28th   *ante diem quintum Kalendas Apriles* or
                 (much more common) *a. d. v Kal. Apr.*

The numbering of the last six months in our calendar recalls the fact that the oldest Roman year, having but ten months, began on March 1st until the time of the Decemviri (450 BC). Before Julius Caesar's reform of the calendar in his capacity as Pontifex Maximus (January 1, 45 BC) the months had 29 days, except the four that had 31 (March, July, October, May) and February, which had 28. After Caesar's reform the number of days in each month became what it still remains. Caesar's reform not only lengthened all the months but also introduced the leap year every four years. It was added by reckoning February 24th twice and not placed at the end of the month for religious reasons. Before Caesar's reform since the year had only 355 days, it was the custom to insert an additional month (the intercalary month) after the feast of Terminus (February 23rd) every other year. But so irregularly had this system been applied by the keepers of the calendar, the pontifices, that by Caesar's and Cicero's time the months had ceased to keep their old places in the seasons.

The old name for the fifth month, Quintilis, was replaced by Julius Caesar in 44 BC to become Iulius. Sextilis was changed to Augustus by the Emperor Octavian Caesar Augustus in 8 BC. A list of the months and their derivations follow:

Ianuarius — from the Italic god Janus
Februarius — from a festival of purification, the Februa
Martius — from Mars, father of the Roman people
Aprilis — from *aperio* 'open'
Maius — from Maia, mother of Mercury

Iunius — from the gens Iulius
Quintilis — the fifth month   Iulius - from the Dictator
Sextilis — the sixth month   Augustus — from the Emperor
September — the seventh month
October — the eighth month
November — the ninth month
December — the tenth month

Variations on the system:

postridie Nonas Maias — on the day *after* the Nones of May
(the *only* exception to the backward reckoning)
tertio die ante Kalendas Septembris — August 29th
V. Idus Novembris = a. d. V Idus Novembris
ex VI Kalendas Decembris - from the sixth day before . . .

IV. The Year

A year is denoted either by giving the names of the consuls or by reckoning the number of years from the traditional date of the founding of Rome (753 B.C.). Both ends are counted — a date B.C. is subtracted from 753, a date A.D. is added to 753.

V. The Time

The day from sunrise to sunset was divided into 12 *horae,* which makes the numbering of hours and the length of each hour depend on the locale. Thus, although the sun might be up for 14 of our hours, it could only be up for 12 Roman hours. This makes references to the time of day in Latin literature difficult, but usually an assumption of a 6 A.M. to 6 P.M. day makes the problem easy. Simply add the time to 6 A.M. and calculate. The night was more simply divided into 4 *vigiliae* (watches) of three hours each, regardless of locale: sunset to 9 P.M.; 9 P.M. to midnight; midnight to 3 A.M.; 3 A.M. to sunrise.

VI. Numerals

The origin of Roman numerals is thus: I was simply a vertical line representing a single finger upheld. II and III indicate two and three fingers. V denotes the opening between the thumb and all the other fingers held pressed together and thus repre-

sents all the five fingers of one hand. Four can be written IIII, representing the four fingers held up, or IV, simply meaning one less than five. Whenever four appears (as in 9 or 14) it can be written as VIIII and XIIII or IX and XIV. VI, VII, etc. are 1 and 2 more than five, etc., X is simply two V's with their angles touching. With the combination of these three simple signs, I, V, X represent all numerals from 1 to 40. For 50 the old Greek symbol for the ch sound, which is Ψ, was used. This was later modified to ⊥ and finally L. 40, therefore, being less than 50, was designated as XL. 100 was also represented by an old Greek symbol, Θ. This was modified to become C. (Another theory is that C is an abbreviation for *centum*.) 1000 was originally Φ, also a Greek symbol, which after some changes developed into ⊕ then M and Ⅽ|Ↄ. (Similarly, it may also be an abbreviation for *mille*.) 500, being half of 1000, was represented by half of the symbol |Ↄ namely D. The remaining Roman numerals were formed by indicating multiplication, as:
10,000 = ⊕ , 100,000 = ⊚   5,000 = Ↄ 50,000 = Ↄ̸
In the late Republic the custom became prevalent to write simple numbers and indicate multiplication by thousands. Thus, $\overline{V}$ = 5000 and $\overline{|XI|}$ = 1,000,000. In Augustan times lines were placed over all numerals for decorative purposes.

VII. Names

The name of a Roman citizen regularly consisted of three parts: the *praenomen* (given name), the *nomen* (name of *gens* or clan), and the *cognomen* (family name). Such a typical name is exemplified by MARCUS TULLIUS CICERO, in which Marcus is the *praenomen,* Tullius the *nomen,* and Cicero the *cognomen.* Sometimes a second *cognomen* (in later Latin called the *agnomen*) is added – especially in honor of military achievements, as in GAIUS CORNELIUS SCIPIO AFRICANUS.

The *praenomina* are usually abbreviated and there are very few of them in Latin:

A. = Aulus	L. = Lucius	Q. = Quintus
App. = Appius	M. = Marcus	Sex. = Sextus
C. or G.= Gaius	M'. = Manius	Ser. = Servius
Cn. = Gnaeus	Mam. = Mamercus	Sp.= Spurius
D. = Decimus	N. = Numerius	T. = Titus
K. = Kaeso	P. = Publius	Ti. = Tiberius

A POMPEIAN SUPPLEMENT:

AN AMERICAN POMPEII

Behold, a little cloud like a man's hand ariseth out of the sea.

I Kings XVIII. 14

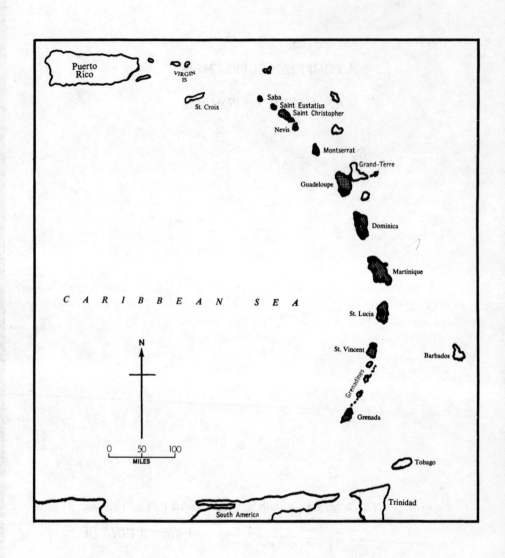

Puerto Rico

VIRGIN IS

St. Croix

Saba
Saint Eustatius
Saint Christopher

Nevis

Montserrat

Grand–Terre

Guadeloupe

Dominica

Martinique

C A R I B B E A N   S E A

St. Lucia

N

St. Vincent

Barbados

Grenadines

0   50   100
MILES

Grenada

Tobago

Trinidad

South America

VOLCANIC ISLANDS OF WEST INDIES

PREFACE

A casual remark about the "American Pompeii" at a morning coffee break furnished the grist for this section, which is at best a supplementary reader to earlier materials on those fine show-pieces of antiquity: Pompeii, Herculaneum, and Stabiae. The utter destruction of St. Pierre, Martinique, in the French West Indies with its population of 30,000 in eight seconds on a May day in the early years of this century ranks this city with the above-mentioned cities in Italy and the newsworthy buried Minoan city on the Aegean isle of Thera as the only highly civil-ized areas in recorded history that have been frozen in time and that are left to posterity to be studied in whatever way.

Vulcanologists place the volcanic action of Mt. Pelée on the isle of Martinique in 1902 only one notch above the violent action of Mt. Vesuvius in 79. Thus there is a close correlation between both places in terms of natural phenomena and the utter destruction left behind. Study of the one enhances the other. Indeed, the classically-steeped world of 1902 did not miss this point, as headlines from all over the world given herein will show. The well-recorded actions of the 1902 eruption, ob-served by an expedition of the National Geographic Society and nicely reported in their scientifically oriented *Magazine* at the time, serve to better inform one how Vesuvius acted in 79 — a matter that is hastily treated in the handbooks on Pompeii and Herculaneum to the detriment of the reader.

This reader is only an introduction to the study of that fatal day for St. Pierre. I have only given headlines to show how a rather confident early 20th century world viewed these events in the usually serene French West Indies. Thus the interested reader may apply to any library with newspaper files of 1902 and read the substance of the articles, which in those days were neatly summarzied in the headlines. A study tour to this de-lightful bit of *la Republique Française* in the Western Hemisphere with the ruins, the volcano (now in slumber), the *Musée Vulcanologique,* and an active tourist board is also to be recommended. Yet, aside from the accounts generated at the time and an article in *American Heritage* for August 1961, the point of departure is the poignant book by two British television writers, Witt & Thomas, who, while doing a series on well-documented natural catastrophes, stopped at St. Pierre and looked behind the headlines. The result was their first book, *The Day the World Ended,* to whose bibliography I owe much. Here is a gripping tale that says much about that strange creature, man. I only hope that your study will be as rewarding as mine has hitherto been.

To Phrontisterion
July MCMLXXII

VOLCANOES

(an article in the July 1902 *National Geographic Magazine)*

There are from 300 to 360 volcanoes on the globe. This estimate includes merely live volcanoes and volcanoes which within recent times have been in action. If we should count the many mountains scattered over the earth which today show signs of volcanic action in a more remote past, the estimate would have to be increased by many hundreds.

Volcanoes would seem to be arranged with more or less symmetry in belts circling the great oceans. A ring of fire surrounds the Pacific. The volcanoes forming this great belt are in places ranged in chains, as along the west coast of Central America and in the Aleutian Islands; elsewhere they are separated by long distances, but nevertheless they would seem to have some connection with each other. Sometimes the line of volcanoes surrounding the Pacific is very narrow, as in Central America, and then again it broadens hundreds of miles, as in the western United States, where extinct volcanoes on the east edge of the belt are hundreds of miles from the ocean and distant from each other. Within this great Pacific circle of volcanoes, 25,000 miles in length, are many volcanic islands.

Eastward from the circle around the Pacific a branch belt extends through Sumatra and Java. On the broken isthmus which ages ago joined Asia and Australia are over 100 volcanoes, many of which are constantly belching forth mud, lava, or ashes. This is the great focus of volcanic action of the earth. Round nearly three sides of the Atlantic basin volcanic districts are scattered with some apparent symmetry. On the west edge of the Atlantic are the volcanoes of the West Indies; but north or south of the Antilles there is not a single volcano on the east coast of America. The volcanic belt of the Mediterranean shore is prolonged to the mountains of Armenia and western Arabia.

Volcanoes may roughly be described as of two types: the expulsive and the explosive. Of the first Hekla in Iceland, Stromboli in Italy, and Mauna Loa in the Hawaiian Islands are good examples. They pour fourth masses of lava which flows like molasses. Of the second type are Vesuvius, Mt. Pelée and the other volcanoes of the West Indies, and those of the Andes and Mexico; these eject the material andesite and are more explosive than those ejecting the ropy lavas.

Perhaps the most probable explanation of explosive eruptions of volcanoes is as follows: the rocks deep beneath the earth's surface are kept moist by the water that seeps slowly through. Probably the rocks contain from 3% to 20% of water. The heat of the molten mass beneath the rocks gradually generates steam, and as time goes on more and more steam is generated. The pressure of this steam is constantly increasing until a time comes when the weight above cannot hold in the expanding force of the steam. Like a boiler the whole mass explodes with terrific fury. An earthquake may open a fissure which by letting down the water rapidly will hasten the explosion; but it is doubtful if an earthquake can do more than this. Water entering by a fissure could hardly invade the vast area upheaved by an explosive eruption.

The Guatemalan earthquake of April probably timed the explosion of Mt. Pelée and La Soufriere. It was the last straw; it brought the last ounce of pressure − one ounce more than the boiler could bear. The local earthquakes in Martinique and St. Vincent were the ruptures and tremors caused by the fettered steam.

National Geographic, June, 1902, p. 204 ff.

ST. PIERRE, THE ACKNOWLEDGED AMERICAN POMPEII

The *Matin* says the disaster is one of the most frightful catastrophes recorded and that one must go back to Pompeii to find a cataclysm of such a calamitous nature. All the newspapers in London express the utmost horror over the Martinique catastrophe, which for its suddenness and magnitude is comparable with that of Pompeii.

It is possible that more lives were lost in the destruction of St. Pierre than when Pompeii and Herculaneum were destroyed. An actual comparison is not possible because the various authorities are unable to do more than guess at the figures in regard to the destruction of the ancient cities. The population of Pompeii at the time of its destruction has been given at from 20,000 to 50,000; but according to Fiorelli Pompeii had no more than 20,000 inhabitants in its earlier days and no more than 12,000 at the time of its destruction. The number of lives lost at Herculaneum is believed to have been considerably less than at Pompeii.

NYTimes 10 May (1902) 1:8

The situation and the lay of the land are not unlike that of the country about Naples. There is the same sweep of bays and terraced hills and the same grim smoking mountain in the background.

J. R. Church, "The Martinique Pompeii" in
Scribner's Magazine, vol. XXXII, July, 1902

The eruption of Pelée throws new light upon the first recorded eruption of Vesuvius and renders intelligible those passages in the Pliny narrative which have heretofore been obscure and thought to be opposed by the facts of geology. The "horrible black cloud" scintillating down the mountain slope and blotting out the landscape is seemingly the absolute counterpart of the great descending black cloud similarly charged with electricity which was the distinctive feature of the Pelée eruption of May 8, 1902.

It was manifestly with the issuance of this cloud that Pompeii

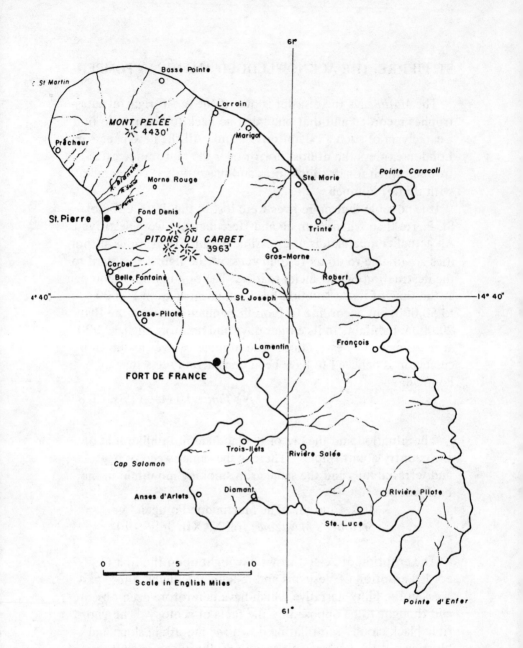

Basse Pointe

C. St Martin

Lorrain

MONT PELÉE
4430'

Marigot

Prêcheur

Morne Rouge

Ste. Marie

Pointe Caracoli

St. Pierre

Fond Denis

Trinté

PITONS DU CARBET
3963'

Gros-Morne

Carbet

Robert

Belle Fontaine

4° 40"

St. Joseph

14° 40"

Case-Pilote

Lamentin

François

FORT DE FRANCE

Trois-Îlets

Rivière Salée

Cap Salomon

Anses d'Arlets

Diamant

Rivière Pilote

Ste. Luce

Pointe d'Enfer

0   5   10

Scale in English Miles

61°

61°

was destroyed, which was therefore on August 25th (not 24th as is generally stated by historians) 79 A.D., as Pliny's narration makes clear that the climax of activity was reached on the second day of the eruption of Vesuvius. Pompeii was not destroyed as a result of incineration (as is generally supposed by geologists and others) but in a manner in all probability closely similar to that which annihilated St. Pierre. The numerous deformed objects of porcelain, glass, etc., which as recovered from Pompeii were thought to represent long periods of time effecting their deformation, have again their exact counterparts in objects recovered from St. Pierre, where the deformation was accomplished in a matter of minutes or seconds.

A. Heilprin's paper in *National Geographic,* Oct. 1904

Tutor in history at the Lycee in St. Pierre, Prof. Roger Bordier, had come to an interesting conclusion. He had found a marked similarity between St. Pierre's predicament and the destruction of Pompeii by Vesuvius in the year 79 A.D. Both towns were ports of the same size; both stood in the shadows of their volcanoes; both had been subjected to a lengthy fallout of ash, cinders, and gases; both had experienced earth tremors.

Only in one fact would Pompeii differ from St. Pierre. In Pompeii nearly all the inhabitants had left the town before it was destroyed. In Pompeii no more than 1000 people had died. It was the indifference of those victims that fascinated Prof. Bordier. He strongly sensed its counterpart in St. Pierre.

Thomas & Witts, *The Day the World Ended, pg. 103*

A DESCRIPTION OF MARTINIQUE (1890)

The first attempt to colonize Martinique was abandoned almost as soon as begun, because the leaders of the expedition found the country "too rugged and too mountainous" and were terrified "by the prodigious number of serpents which covered its soil." Landing on June 25, 1635, Olive and Duplessis left the island after a few hours' observation and made sail for Guadeloupe. Martinique was later settled by the French in 1655 and with the exception of 22 years (1794-1816), when the English held it, has been a colony ever since.* It sends a senator and two deputies to the National Assembly in Paris.

Although less than 50 miles in extreme length and less than 20 in average breadth, there are upward of 400 mountains on this little island. These again are divided and interpeaked and bear hillocks on their slopes, and the lowest hillock on Martinique is 50 metres high. Some of the peaks are said to be totally inaccessible; many more are so on one or even three sides. Ninety-one only of the principal mountains have been named.

Is the great volcano dead? Nobody knows. Less than 40 years ago (1852) it rained ashes over the roofs of St. Pierre; within 20 years it has muttered utterings. For the moment it appears to be asleep, and the clouds have dripped into the cup of its highest crater until it has become a lake several hundreds of yards in circumference. The crater occupied by this lake, called L'Etang ("the Pool"), has never been active within human memory. There are others — difficult and dangerous to visit because they open on the side of a tremendous gorge — and it was one of these, no doubt, which has always been called La Soufrière ("the Sulphur"), which rained ashes over the city in 1852.

The explosion was almost concomitant with the last of a series of earthquake shocks, which began in the middle of May and which ended in the first week in August. In the village of Au Precheur, lying at the foot of the west slope of Pelée the people had for some time been complaining of an oppressive stench of

*In 1946 under the new Constitution of the French Republic the isle of Martinique as well as its other component in the French West Indies became an overseas part of metropolitan France like a state in our Union. At that time these areas ceased to issue their own postage stamps.

sulphur, when on August 4th much trepidation was caused by a long and appalling noise from the mountain. These sounds continued through intervals until the following night, sometimes deepening into a rumble like thunder. At 11 P.M. the noise was terrible enough to fill all St. Pierre with alarm, and on the morning of the 6th the city presented an unwonted aspect of a great hoar-frost.

St. Pierre is the quaintest, queerest, and the prettiest withal among West Indian cities — all stone-built and stone-flagged with very narrow streets, wooden or zinc awnings, and peaked roofs of red tile, pierced by gabled dormers. Most of the buildings are painted in a clear, yellow tone, which contrasts delightfully with the burning blue ribbon of tropical sky above, and no street is absolutely level; nearly all of them climb hills, descend into hollows, curve, twist, and describe sudden angles. There is everywhere a loud murmur of running water, pouring through the deep gutters contrived between the paved thoroughfare and the absurd little sidewalks, varying in width from one to three feet. The architecture is that of the 17th century and reminds one of the antiquated French Quarter of New Orleans. All the tints, the forms, the vistas would seem to have been especially selected or designed for aquarelle studies. The windows are frameless openings without glass; some have iron bars; all have heavy wooden shutters with moveable slats, through which light and air can enter.

Lafcadio Hearn, *Two Years in the French West Indies,* 1890, pp. 214-6.

LIFE IMMEDIATELY BEFORE THE CATASTROPHE

A true picture of conditions in St. Pierre in its last days is given in the two sets of items published below. The first is a letter written by Mrs. Thomas Prentis, wife of the American consul in St. Pierre, who perished with her family, to her sister-in-law in Melrose, Massachusetts, on April 25, 1902. This was one of the last letters out of the city and was published in the

Boston Post on May 10, 1902, when the world at last found out
about the occurrences on a small West Indian isle. The Pren-
tises made their residence in Melrose but had been in Martinique
for a year and before that had spent 20 years in the isle of
Mauritius in the Indian Ocean. A simple memorial to this family
stands on the balcony facing the sea by the Musée Vulcanologique.

The second and lengthy but interesting item is a series of extracts about Pelee's activity taken from St. Pierre's daily newspaper, *Les Colonies.* The words speak badly for the editor,
whose folly cost him his life. The preservation of the papers is
due to the thought and diligence of the chaplain of the USS
Dixie, the rescue ship despatched immediately by President
Theodore Roosevelt to Martinique after the disaster on behalf of
the French Government. Rev. J. F. MacGrail made a most careful
and exhausting search for copies of *Les Colonies,* a local newspaper with small circulation outside St. Pierre, where all copies
had been destroyed. The collection constitutes an historical
document of rare importance and interest. The chaplain made
his partial translations available for immediate press release and
later published the entire translation in the *Century Magazine*
for August 1902.

MRS. PRENTIS' LETTER

My dear Sister,

This morning the whole population of the city is on the alert,
and every eye is directed toward Mt. Pelée, an extinct volcano.
Everybody is afraid that the volcano has taken into its head to
burst forth and destroy the whole island. Fifty years ago Mt.
Pelée burst forth before with terrific force and destroyed everything for a radius of several miles. For several days the mountain has been bursting forth, and immense quantities of lava are
flowing down the side of the mountain.

All the inhabitants are going up to see it. There is not a horse
to be had on the island. Those belonging to the natives are kept
in readiness to leave at a moment's notice. Last Wednesday,
which was April 23, I was in my room with little Christine, and
we heard three distinct shocks. They were so great that we sup-

posed at first that there was someone at the door and Christine went and found no one there. The first report was very loud, but the second and third were so great that dishes were thrown from the shelves and the house was completely rocked.

We can see Mt. Pelée from the rear windows in our house, and although it is fully four miles away, we can hear the roar and see the fire and lava issuing from it with terrific force. The city is covered with ashes, and clouds of smoke have been over our heads for the past five days. The smell of sulphur is so strong that the horses on the street stop and snort, and some of them are obliged to give up, drop in their harness, and die from suffocation. Many of the people are obliged to wear wet handkerchiefs over their faces to protect them from the strong fumes of sulphur.

My husband assures me that there is no immediate danger, and when there is the least particle of danger, he will leave the place. There is an American schooner, the *E. J. Morse,* in the harbor and will remain here for at least two weeks. If the volcano becomes very bad, we shall embark at once and go out to sea. The papers in this city are asking if we are going to experience another earthquake and volcano similar to that which struck here some 50 years ago.

EXTRACTS FROM *LES COLONIES*

THURSDAY, May 1   In the ECHOES column – the sole
                                            reference

Many persons at St. Pierre affirm that the day before yesterday between 3 and 5 o'clock in the afternoon they felt several shocks of earthquake.

FRIDAY, May 2   It never occurred.

We remind our readers that the grand excursion to Mont Pelée organized by the Members of La Societé Gymnastique et de Tir will take place next Sunday, May 4. Those who have never enjoyed the panorama offered to the view of the astonished spectator at a height of 1300 meters, and those who desire to see at

close range the still yawning hole from which in the last few days
thick clouds of smoke have escaped (much to the consternation
of the inhabitents of Precheur and Ste. Philomene) should profit
by this fine opportunity and register their names this evening at
latest at the society's headquarters in the Rue Longchamps.
The meeting of the excursionists will be at the Marche du
Fort at 3:15 in the morning, and the departure for Mont
Pelée will be at 3:30 exactly.

SATURDAY, May 3   A letter from Hey-Pet

Yesterday the people of St. Pierre were treated again to a
grandiose spectacle in the majesty of the smoking volcano.
It would seem that many signs ought really to have warned
us that Mont Pelée was in a state of genuine and serious eruption. Thursday night the Rivière Blanche, which was rolling
masses of black mud, threatened an overflow. There were
several slight earthquake shocks. Detonations were also heard,
and the rattlings of stones cast forth by the crater. While at
St. Pierre the admirers of the beautiful could not take their
eyes from the smoke column of the volcano and timid people
were commending their souls to God, very different things
were happening on the heights.

Last night's eruption

Yesterday the volcano's cinders fell lightly at Abymes and
Precheur and as far as Rivière Blanche. During the night this
ashen rain grew so much denser that at about 2 o'clock the
city looked as if there had been a fall of snow.

The illusion was complete. St. Pierre was in a state of agitation. One could hear everywhere through the night voices
as at the time of a nocturnal earthquake. The older inhabitants immediately recalled the eruption of 1852; the younger
generation went into admiration over a spectacle so absolutely
new to them.

A dust as fine as millers' grist had by this time sifted into
every room and over every piece of furniture. There was
coughing and sneezing on every side. Fort has a deeper coat-
ing than Centre and Mouillage. By 6 o'clock in the morning
the ashes were already a centimeter thick; they were soon

108

two centimeters thick. Brooms were plied without ceasing.

The cinder rain never stops. At about 9:30 the sun shines forth timidly. The passing of carriages no longer resounds through our streets. The wheels are muffled. The old trucks creak along languidly on their worn tires. Gusts of wind bring ashes down from the roofs and awnings and blow them into rooms wherever windows imprudently have been left open. Shops which had unclosed their doors half-way are now barred up securely.

Last night Père Mary threw open the church. A large crowd of people assembled there precipitately and received communion. The sea is black. The rivers are full of muddy water. It is going to be difficult to feed the people.

In the ECHOES column

The excursion which had been organized for tomorrow morning will not leave St. Pierre, the crater being absolutely inaccessible. Those who were to have joined the party will be notified later on when it will be found practicable to carry out the original plan.

Reprinted from the *Official Bulletin* of 1852

The rest of the night was passed in the greatest anxiety. Lighted torches could be seen moving rapidly on the different hills; people were fleeing along the highroad, announcing that they were going to the churches of the city to implore the Divine mercy. No one knew what had happened. To every inquiry the answer was: "La Soufrière is boiling."

When the morning dawned, we found that St. Pierre had been no less frightened than we. The noise had been heard by many, and, on awaking in the morning, St. Pierre had found the roofs of houses, the pavements of the streets, the leaves of the trees covered with a light layer of gray cinders which gave to the city the aspect of some European town silvered over with the first frosts of autumn. This cinder fall also covered the countryside between St. Pierre and Mont Pelée, Morne Rouge, and even Carbet. The river called Rivière Blanche no longer deserved its name. Its waters were as black as a solution of cinders or slate, and their trace at the mouth of the river could be seen far out at sea, as happens after great floods.

SUNDAY, May 4 — no edition on Sunday

MONDAY, May 5 — Amidst the electioneering in lower right corner

Communication by land was no easier yesterday. Many excursionists who had started afoot and on horseback were compelled to turn back. After 3 o'clock in the afternoon communication ceased between the customs-service posts of St. Pierre and Precheur. The rain of cinders began at about 4 o'clock in the evening. Everyone in that quarter passed the night in mortal fear.

The sea in places is covered with dead birds. Many lie asphyxiated along the roads. The cattle are also suffering greatly, being asphyxiated by the cinder dust. Children of cultivators are wandering aimlessly like little human wrecks about the countryside with their little donkeys. A group of them goes hesitatingly down the Rue Victor Hugo. They are no longer black, but white. They look as if a hoar-frost had fallen over them.

Since 2:30 o'clock Saturday the steamers of the Compagnie Girard have been crowded at every trip. Many families from the neighboring countryside, not feeling that they would be safe in St. Pierre, are leaving for Ft. de France and the south. All schools were dismissed Saturday. We may observe in passing that in the eruption of 1851 the cinder rain did not extend so far. This morning the rivers that flow near the city and that have their springs in the southern slope of Mont Pelée are blackish and overflow their banks. It is believed that this superabundance of water is ejected by the crater forming a siphon with the sea.

Most of the shops in St. Pierre were open this morning, but the town does not yet wear its customary aspect. There is uneasiness everywhere to be felt and a certain apprehension. It is very difficult to expose merchandise on account of the ashes that that fall from roofs and awnings.

In the ECHOES column

On the Rue Macary at Fort about 2½ kilos of cinders have fallen to the square meter. The country in the Rivière Blanche valley must have received 4 times as much. On Saturday the sidewalks of Rue Hurtault were covered with a layer 3 centimeters deep. A violent freshet of Rivière Blanche at 8 A.M. has just been reported. The old bridge has been carried away. The river is full of bodies of dead animals.

Cable Despatches

Mont Pelée seems this morning to have entered into a period of calm. Cinders continue to fall at Precheur and at other places to leeward of the craters. Three tenths of a millimeter of cinders have fallen at St. Pierre during the night, which makes a total of 4 millimeters of cinders for this city.

The country is deserted, owing to the complete lack of food and drink. Animals are dying of hunger and thirst; branches are breaking off the trees under the weight of the cinder fall. Last night there was renewed intensity of the phenomena of the eruption with great discharges of atmospheric electricity, thunder, and lightning, and tongues of fire. Cinders fell in showers during the night on Macouba. At the last moment we hear that Rivière Blanche is rising extraordinarily and threatening the Guerin works.

Latest

At 12:55 P.M. the sea withdrew about 100 meters from the shore and then rushed back upon the beach. Agitation is extreme. Thousands are running toward the village. The air is full of the cries of women and children. Shops are being closed in haste. The steamer *Topaze* and some pirogues grounded on the coast, but the steamer manages to haul off again. A strong southwester is blowing. There is universal consternation.

The Guerin factory has been swept over by the sea. Evidently this is the result of seismic action. 1:45 P.M. The Usine Guerin is said to be destroyed. Many deaths are reported.

TUESDAY, May 6   The Day's Panic

At the moment of the catastrophe at the Guerin works a great volume of smoke, which people found it difficult to account for, was visible at St. Pierre. "The works are on fire," said some. "A crater has opened at that point," said others. The crowds which the enormous wave had drawn together in the streets and on the shore were running to this side and that in extraordinary agitation. The women especially seemed to have escaped from a madhouse.

A human flood poured up from the depths of Mouillage. It was a flight for safety without knowing where to return. The whole city is on foot. Doors of ships and private homes are closing. Everyone is preparing to take refuge on the heights.

The city in darkness

To complete the confusion in St. Pierre, the city was plunged in darkness. The electric plant would not work last night. Some persons have thought that the failure came from a diminution in the outflow of the water of the Morestin, and therefore was due to insufficient pressure of water. It took but little more to suppose that the Morestin might run dry entirely, hence an increase in the panic.

In reality the sudden failure of the electric service is due to the atmospheric conditions into which St. Pierre has been plunged ever since the eruption of Mont Pelée has attained its present proportions.

The night's panic

People slept with one eye open, dreading a new catastrophe in the night, and darkness adding to the terror. Toward 2 A.M. there were terrific mutterings like those of thunder in a great storm. The dwellers at Fort thought another lava wave had burst from the crater and that Fort River would overflow. Rue Levassor was in an indescribable commotion. All began to move out. The noise (the broken fragments of conversation in the night) increased the alarm.

In the Rue Victor Hugo there were people at all the windows, calling out to know what had happened. Some replied that it was the Roxelane that had leaped from its banks, others that it was the Peres River. The streets of Mouillage were invaded by crowds without a place for their heads. In fact, the alarm was

112

not justified. We heard someone at about 5 A.M. remark from a window: "We can get no sleep while the volcano sleeps so soundly that he snores." That man was a philosopher.

WEDNESDAY, May 7   An interview with M. Landes

It would seem that the central orifice of the volcano, situated in the higher fissures, was emitting in larger quantities than ever, albeit intermittently, dusty masses of a black and yellow substance. It would be safer to leave the lower valleys and live at a certain elevation, if one wished to be sure of escaping the fate of Pompeii and Herculaneum and not be submerged by muddy lava. "But," adds M. Landes, "Vesuvius has never made many victims. Pompeii was evacuated in time, and few bodies have ever been found in the buried cities. CONCLUSION: Mont Pelée is no more to be feared by St. Pierre than Vesuvius is feared by Naples.

The city's rivers

Yesterday at about 7 o'clock in the evening the waters of the Peres River increased in volume. Everyone supposed the rise had been simply due to the rains. Suddenly, however, a torrent bore down, bringing with it great quantities of bamboo branches. Then came trees and large blocks of stone, which may still be seen in the bed of the river. The bridge at Perrinelle Place has disappeared under the rocks. If the wall of the dwelling had not been so massive, the stables would have gone down the torrent. This first overflow lasted until about 10 o'clock and then diminished. The water rose again at about 2 o'clock in the morning.

At the mouth of the river the water is engulfed in an enormous hole which it has dug out here. Into this hole the flood precipitates all the vegetable and mineral debris it has torn up along its course. A little out to sea the current comes up to the surface again, still laden with the drifting wreckage.

The Roxelane also overflowed suddenly at 7 o'clock yesterday evening. This rise was caused solely by the heavy rains on the heights. The water holds in suspension all the ashes it amasses on its way, and it is therefore very dark. At the river's mouth great quantities of dead fish were found.

The panic at St. Pierre

The departures from St. Pierre are increasing in numbers
From morning to night and even during the night one sees
hurrying people, carrying packages, trunks, and children. The
steamers of the Compagnie Girard are never empty. We confess
that we cannot understand this panic. Where could one be
better off than at St. Pierre?

The Volcano Commissioners

FORT DE FRANCE, May 7 (10 A.M.) — The governor has ap-
pointed a commission to study the nature of the Mont Pelée
eruption. The commission is composed of the following gentle-
men: Lieutenant Colonel Gerbault, chief of artillery and president of the commission; M. Mirville, head chemist of the
colonial troops; M. Leonce, assistant engineer of colonial roads
and bridges; and MM. Doze and Landes, professors of natural
sciences at the Lycée of St. Pierre. The public will be kept informed of the results of the commissioners' investigations.

The last words from the ECHOES column

Thursday being the feast of the Ascension, the stenographic
courses are postponed until next Thursday, May 15.
The adult course, which was to have taken place Friday next,
is likewise postponed till May 15.
Our offices being closed tomorrow, our next number will not
appear until Friday.

THURSDAY, May 8   Ascension Day and a Date with Destiny

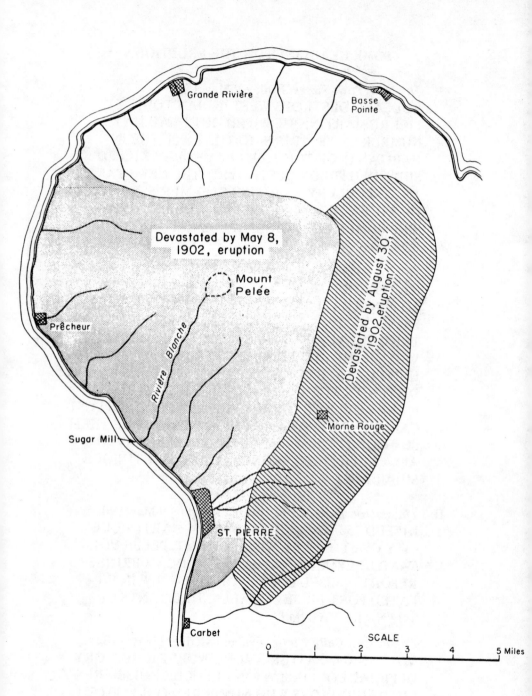

Grande Rivière

Basse
Pointe

Devastated by May 8,
1902, eruption

Mount
Pelée

Devastated by August 30,
1902, eruption

Prêcheur

Rivière Blanche

Morne Rouge

Sugar Mill

ST. PIERRE

Carbet

SCALE

| 0 | 1 | 2 | 3 | 4 | 5 Miles |

115

SOME HEADLINES ON THE ERUPTION

I. *The New York Times* Friday 9 May 1902
VOLCANO DESTROYS WEST INDIAN TOWN ST.
PIERRE MARTINIQUE WIPED OUT DEAD MAY
NUMBER 25,000 IT IS SAID THAT ALL THE IN-
HABITANTS OF THE TOWN HAVE BEEN KILLED
SHIPS IN HARBOR DESTROYED THE NEWS TAKEN
TO ST. LUCIA BY A BRITISH STEAMER SEVENTEEN
OF WHOSE MEN WERE KILLED QUEBEC STEAM-
SHIP COMPANY'S RORAIMA LOST WITH ALL ON
BOARD

The New York Times Saturday 10 May 1902
MARTINIQUE DEAD MAY NUMBER 40,000 EFFORTS
TO PENETRATE INTO ST. PIERRE FAIL WARSHIP
SAVES 30 LIVES SO FAR AS IS KNOWN THESE ARE
THE ONLY SURVIVORS GOVERNOR PROBABLY A
VICTIM THE KILLED ALSO BELIEVED TO INCLUDE
UNITED STATES CONSUL PRENTIS AND HIS FAMILY
DISTRICTS WITHIN A FOUR-MILE RADIUS OF ST.
PIERRE OVERWHELMED EIGHTEEN VESSELS LOST
CABLE REPAIR STEAMER GRAPPIER ONE OF THEM
SOME OF THE RORAIMA'S PASSENGERS SAVED
ALL CABLE LINES BROKEN THINK MARTINIQUE
SUBMERGED

II. *The Boston Daily Globe* Friday Morning 9 May 1902
KILLED 25,000 SUCH TALE FROM MARTINIQUE
CITY OF ST. PIERRE WIPED OUT MT. PELÉE VOL-
CANO IN ERUPTION STEAMER RODDAM BRINGS
REPORT VESSEL LOST 17 OF HER CREW IN ILL-
FATED PORT BELIEVED ALL INHABITANTS OF
TOWN ARE VICTIMS

The Boston Daily Globe Friday Evening 9 May 1902
VOLCANIC DISASTER AMONG WORST IN HISTORY
OFFICIAL CONFIRMATION FRENCH CRUISER RES-
CUED SURVIVORS WHO NUMBERED ONLY 30 OUT
OF 25,000 POPULATION

116

The Boston Daily Globe Saturday 10 May 1902
ST. PIERRE HORROR GROWS APACE NOT A SINGLE
SURVIVOR FROM LAND LAVA FLOOD DID AWFUL
WORK IN THREE MINUTES ST. PIERRE CHIEF CITY
OF MARTINIQUE IS NO MORE NO SURVIVOR
KNOWN TO HAVE ESCAPED FROM CITY

III. *The Boston Post* Friday 9 May 1902
ST. PIERRE DESTROYED 20,000 REPORTED LOST
CHIEF CITY OF MARTINIQUE SAID TO HAVE BEEN
OVERWHELMED BY VOLCANOES BUILDINGS RAZED
& BURIED BENEATH LAVA SHIPPING IN HARBOR
DESTROYED

The Boston Post Saturday 10 May 1902
DEAD AT ST. PIERRE NOW PLACED AT 40,000
DESTRUCTION OF CITY AND SHIPPING IN HARBOR
REPORTED COMPLETE NOTHING LIVING LEFT
WITHIN FOUR-MILE RADIUS OF BURNING VOLCANO

The Boston Post Sunday 11 May 1902
NO ONE ALIVE AT ST. PIERRE A BRITISH SHIP
TRIES TO ATTRACT ATTENTION FAILS TO DIS-
COVER A SINGLE HUMAN BEING ALIVE DEATH
ESTIMATE REMAINS AT 40,000 NO SIGN OF LIFE AT
ST. PIERRE FOODSTUFFS OF ALL KINDS NEEDED
SURVIVORS ARRIVE AT FORT DE FRANCE ISLAND
OF ST. VINCENT LAID WASTE VOLCANIC ACTIVI-
TIES IN DOMINICA

IV. *The Boston Evening Transcript* Friday 9 May 1902
WHOLE CITY PERISHED ST. PIERRE MARTINIQUE
HAS BEEN OVERWHELMED MT. PELEE VOLCANO
CAUSED TERRIBLE CATASTROPHE BLOW FELL AT
EIGHT YESTERDAY MORNING FRENCH NAVAL
CAPTAIN DESPAIRS OF ENTIRE POPULATION HE
REPORTS RESCUING ONLY ABOUT 30 SURVIVORS
PEOPLE OF ILL-FATED TOWN NUMBERED ABOUT
25,000 ERUPTION CONTINUES AFTER DESTROYING
CITY

The Boston Evening Transcript Saturday 10 May 1902
ST. PIERRE HORROR GROWS VOLCANIC ERUPTION
CONTINUES IN MARTINIQUE GREAT ANXIETY
EXISTS FOR BRITISH ISLAND OF ST. VINCENT
SERIOUS ACTIVITIES OF ITS VOLCANO SOUFRIERE
MT. PELÉE'S VICTIMS CERTAINLY NUMBERED BY
THOUSANDS HOPE THAT MORE THAN REPORTED
HAVE ESCAPED ONLY FRAGMENTARY NEWS FROM
STRICKEN ANTILLES DETAILS MUST AWAIT RE-
PAIR OF BROKEN CABLES

PRESIDENT THEODORE ROOSEVELT'S PROCLAMATION ON THE ST. PIERRE DISASTER

One of the greatest calamities in history has fallen upon our
neighboring island of Martinique. The Consul of the United
States at Guadeloupe has telegraphed from Fort de France under
date of yesterday that the disaster is complete, that the city of
St. Pierre has ceased to exist, and that the American consul and
his family have perished. He is informed that 30,000 people
have lost their lives, that 50,000 are homeless and hungry, that
there is urgent need of all kinds of provisions, and that the visit
of vessels for the work of supply and rescue is imperatively
required.

The government of France, while expressing its thanks for
the marks of sympathy which have reached it from America,
informs us that Fort de France and the entire island of Martinique is still threatened. They therefore request that for the purpose of rescuing the people who are in such deadly peril and
threatened with starvation the government of the United States
send as soon as possible the means of transporting them from
the stricken island. The island of St. Vincent and perhaps others
in that region are also seriously menaced by the calamity which
has taken so appalling a form in Martinique.

I have directed the Departments to take such measures for
the relief of these stricken people as lies within the executive
discretion, and I earnestly commend this case of unexampled
disaster to the generous consideration of the Congress. For this
purpose I recommend that an appropriation of $500,000 be
made to be immediately available.

118

A RETROSPECT: THE VICAR-GENERAL'S LETTER

At the very beginning of the disturbances on Mont Pelée which resulted in the destruction of St. Pierre on May 8, the Bishop of Martinique, Monseigneur de Cormont, was in Paris. The historic letter (in the form of a journal from May 2 to May 21) below was written to him in French by the Very Rev. G. Parel, Vicar-General and Administrator (Acting Bishop) of the Diocese of Martinique, by whom a copy was given to the earlier-mentioned chaplain of the US Dixie, Rev. J. F. MacGrail, in response to a request for information concerning the disaster during the ship's relief visit to Fort-de-France, Martinique, in the latter part of May. It is perhaps not too much to say that this narrative is indispensable to the history of those days. It recalls the less detailed account by Pliny the Younger of the great eruption of Vesuvius and suggests the record that Pliny the Elder might have made, had he survived the disaster. The translation of Miss Alice Gorren was published in the *Century Magazine* for August 1902 and is here produced in full except for those parts that apply to ecclesiastical business or which are just too gory.

Fort-de-France, May, 1902

Monseigneur,

A catastrophe such as that which has befallen us was never before heard of. It has no parallel in history. Yet, in the midst of our great dismay and the confusion that surrounds us, I should like to give you a brief account of events as they have happened and are happening day by day.

You are familiar with the configuration of Mont Pelée (4428 ft.) You know that it dominates the entire northern part of the island and that it is the starting point of numerous narrow valleys and of many torrents, here somewhat inaccurately called rivers. These valleys and rivers stretch out in every direction from St. Pierre to Grande Anse. The highest peak of the mountain is Morne Lacroix, which can be seen distinctly from St. Pierre on clear days and at the foot of which lies the ancient crater that is known as Etang Sec ("Dry Pond") in contrast to the lake situated on the opposite slope of the same peak, the waters of which are always high.

FRIDAY, April 25: On the morning of April 25, although the weather was very clear, the summit of the mountain wore a splendid cap of white vapors. I was able to enjoy this spectacle (I had been at St. Pierre since the night before) in taking the 6:30 P.M. boat to return home. When I reached Fort-de-France, the despatches had already announced a volcanic eruption. Everyone was deeply interested, and excursionists set out immediately for the crater, quiescent for centuries except that in 1851 it had thrown out a harmless shower of ashes, which had fallen upon St. Pierre overnight. The fathers of our college were not the last to reach the mountain. From the summit of Morne Lacroix they could discern that Etang Sec, which has the shape of an immense basin inclined toward St. Pierre, was filling up with boiling water that gave out the strong smell of sulphur.

FRIDAY, May 2: Eight days later the nature of the eruption had changed. The volcano now emitted cinders instead of vapor. At 11:30 that night St. Pierre was awakened by the noise of terrifying detonations and beheld one of the most stupendous of natural spectacles: a volcano in full eruption, sending forth an enormous column of black smoke, which rose into the sky jagged through by flashes of lightning and accompanied by formidable explosions. A few moments later a shower of cinders descended on the town, extending though with less density as far as Ft.-de-France and over the entire island.

SATURDAY, May 3: When it awoke Saturday morning, the whole colony saw cinders scattered everywhere, even in the interior of houses. Another despatch, even more alarming than that of the night before, having come to me from Le Precheur I left at 8 o'clock for St. Pierre, which I found covered with cinders, as if a grayish snow had fallen. The black smoke of the volcano ascended in opaque clouds. Every six hours its cannonading redoubled in intensity. Under a rain of cinders from which came the same strong sulphurous smell I visited Ste. Philomene, Le Precheur, and Morne Rouge, towns nearest the volcano. These three places were filled with people from the country fleeing from the hills to the coast. The churches, which had been thrown open all night, were emptied of their congregations. I did what I could to reassure the people. In returning from Le Precheur, I was enveloped in a cloud of cinders so thick that the darkness fell like night. During the afternoon in the midst of a ceremony at the cathedral there was a terrible panic.

SUNDAY, May 4: On that day, the wind having changed, the shower of ashes took a northerly direction and fell at Ajoupa-Bouillon, Basse-Pointe, Macouba and Grand Rivière; St. Pierre breathed more freely.

MONDAY, May 5: Since the morning Rivière Blanche, so called because of the milky iridescence of its waters and which for some days had been swelling to disquieting proportions (although there had been no rain), had assumed suddenly the aspect of a menacing and muddy torrent, the violence of which attracted the curious. At the same time a moving column of vapor was seen in the high valley that extends from the crater. Some said that a new crater was forming, but this proved not to be the case. It was an avalanche of black and smoking mud, ejected by the crater and swollen by successive discharges, until it became a rolling mountain (though still an invisible one), while it was breaking its way through the deep gorge. The moment it approached the delta where the Guerin factory stood, its presence was betrayed by the ascending vapors and by a great noise. The few persons who witnessed the sight quickly raised the cry: "Run for your life." Too late! In the twinkling of an eye the works, the villas of the owners, the houses of the workmen were engulfed. The avalanche spread its incandescent mud several meters deep over an area several hundred meters in extent and even to the small hills nearby. M. Guerin fils, his wife, M. duQuesne, the head overseer, and 25 employees or domestics were buried under the mass. Nothing but the smokestack of the works, a little bent to one side, remains to tell the tale of the disaster. This was about noon.

At the same time in the roadstead of St. Pierre the sea withdrew, as if affrighted. The steamboat *Girard* of the Fort-de-France service was left on the bottom by the receding water; then suddenly the sea returned in a tidal wave that swept the Place Bertin and the first streets beyond and spread terror throughout the city, so that people began to flee to the hills. Twenty minutes later all was calm again. When news of this reached Fort-de-France, the governor immediately called the *Suchet* into service to take him to the scene of the disaster. I requested permission to join him, but my request was politely refused, as it was feared that my presence might increase the panic.

TUESDAY, May 6: I was therefore not able to leave until the following morning by the ordinary 8 o'clock boat. Accompanied by Abbe Le Breton, I went to Rivière Blanche. It was a roaring torrent, rolling rocks, tree trunks, and smoking mud onward in its crashing course. With its streaming line of smoke it resembled a locomotive rushing headlong into the sea.

I could see the sides of the crater covered with rocks and mud and dug into vertical grooves by the waters pouring out from its mouth. Two peaks which seemed to frame the crater formed for it an advanced valley, and into this the waters gathered and then precipitated themselves into zigzags into the foaming torrent that passed before us.

WEDNESDAY, May 7: At 4 o'clock in the morning I was awakened in my room by loud detonations, and I beheld a display of lightning comparable only to some stupendous exhibition of fireworks. Sometimes it was a fiery crescent seeming to glide over the surface of the crater, sometimes perpendicular gashes of light rent the column of smoke, sometimes a fringe of fire encircled the dense coils rolling above the furnace of the crater. Two red craters like fire-filled caldrons or blast furnaces were visible during half an hour, one (that at the right) a little higher than the other.

I could distinguish clearly four different types of sounds: first, the claps of thunder following about 20 seconds after the lightning; then the muffled, powerful explosions of the volcano like the firing of many cannon together; third, the continual rumbling of the crater, which has been likened in the city to the roaring of a lion; and finally, as the bass note of this sinister harmony, the mighty noise of overflowing waters, produced by the rising, beyond anything that has ever been known, of all the torrents issuing from the mountain. This enormous rising of 30 streams at once without a drop of rain having fallen near the coast gives an idea of the cataracts that must pour down upon the summit from the rain clouds attracted by the crater.

When daylight broke over the roadstead of St. Pierre, there was one great cry of stupefaction: it was completely covered

122

as far as the eye could see with little floating islands — the wreckage of field and forest, trunks of gigantic trees, pumice stones, flotsam and jetsam of all sorts, carried down by the streams. The mouths of the rivers, gnawed away by the impetuous rush of the waters, disappeared in the sea, and all those black and turbid torrents, mixing with the sea's waves, tinged them for a space with a little yellowish line, which ceased abruptly, as though every torrent had been drifting molten lead. Everything on this fateful eve was extraordinary.

I had taken with me Père Ackermann and Père Fuzier, and in a rowboat we made our way not without danger through the wreckage of the roadstead toward Ste. Philomene and Precheur. All the bridge crossings of the road that skirts the shore had been carried away . . . Half of the inhabitants had taken refuge at St. Pierre, where the barracks and schools had been thrown open to them by order of the governor. As for me, I resisted the urgent wish expressed that I should remain, thinking it to be my duty to be at home for the Ascension, and I left St. Pierre by the 2:30 o'clock boat with a promise that I would return the following evening or at latest Friday morning. The boat was crowded with fugitives from St. Pierre. I stepped out of the rowboat that had brought me from Le Precheur just in time to get on board. Was it my good angel protecting me? Or rather would it not have been better for me not to survive but to die?

THURSDAY, May 8, The Ascension: This day should be written in blood.

Toward 4 o'clock in the morning a violent thunder storm with torrents of rain broke over Fort-de-France. Toward 8 o'clock the horizon in the north in the direction of the volcano was as black as ink. The clouds were moving rapidly toward the northwest. The sky was darkening more and more, when I heard suddenly something like hail falling on the roofs and the leaves of the trees. A great noise rose from the city. In church, where the 8 o'clock mass was in progress, a terrible panic seized the congregation, and the priest was left standing alone. Night had descended on us, and the crash of thunder was continuous. The sea retreated three times for a distance of several hundred meters. The boat which was putting out for St. Pierre turned back.

I stepped out on my balcony to take in the situation, and immediately it was covered with a hail of stones and still hot cinders. People stood petrified on their door steps. Others ran wildly here and there through the streets. All this lasted for about a quarter hour — a quarter hour of horror.

But what was happening at St. Pierre? No one dared to think. Telephonic communication had been cut off abruptly in the middle of a word. Some persons asserted that they had seen above the tops of the mountains separating us from St. Pierre a column of fire rising into the sky and spreading outward toward all points of the horizon. Boundless anxiety seized upon us all. At 11 o'clock the *Marin* set out to reconnoiter. It witnessed a sight appalling beyond imagination. St. Pierre was nothing but one vast brazier. When the truth reached us about 1 o'clock, a cry of horror went up not to be described.

I learn that a boat is to be sent out to rescue the wounded. I am fortunate enough to obtain a place in it together with one of my vicars. The police and gendarmes cannot keep back the crowd struggling to make its way on board. People refuse to believe in the reality of so horrible a disaster. They cling to every hypothesis that may still make hope possible. We say to ourselves that at least a great part of the population must have had time to flee.

When at about 4 o'clock in the afternoon we turn the last promontory that separates us from what was once the magnificent panorama of St. Pierre, the first sight that strikes our eyes at the farther end of the roadstead is Rivière Blanche with its stream of smoke throwing itself furiously as the day before into the sea. Then a little further out a large steamer, the *Roraima,* in flames. We hear that it is an American packet, just arrived that morning, in time to be enveloped in the catastrophe. Two other steamboats are burning nearer the shore. Wreckage and the upturned keels of boats strew the roadstead. And this is all that is left of the 30 or 40 ships anchored here the day previous. All along the quays for a distance of 200 meters piles of lumber are burning. There are smaller fires on the hills about the city visible through the smoke as far as Fonds Core. But St. Pierre, that city this morning alive, full of human souls is no more! It lies consumed before us in its winding-sheet of smoke and cinders, silent and desolate, a city of the dead. We strain our eyes for fleeing inhabitants, for men returning to bury their lost ones.

We see no one! There is no living being left in this desert of desolation, framed in a terrifying solitude. In the background when the cloud of smoke and cinders breaks away, the mountain and its slopes, once so green, stand forth like an Alpine landscape. They look as if they were covered with a thick coat of snow, and through the thickened atmosphere rays of pale sunshine, wan and unknown to our latitudes, illumine this scene with a light that seems to belong to the other side of the grave.

In the face of this desert the company of soldiers sent out for the rescue could have nothing to do. We returned utterly cast down to Carbet. There new emotions, indescribable scenes, awaited us. In one house 15 dead bodies lay heaped in a mass. Elsewhere were dying men shockingly burned. The *Suchet* and the *Pouyer-Quertier* come to our assistance. We get into Fort-de-France at 10 o'clock that night.

It is time to explain to ourselves how the frightful catastrophe took place. That is not so easy as it would seem; in the first place, because none struck by the scourge has lived to tell of it, and, secondly, because those who were saved by finding themselves on its confines do not entirely agree in their descriptions, having been doubtless too profoundly agitated by the sights they witnessed. This however is what I have gathered as being certain.

The rumbling of the volcano had become more alarming, and the ejections of cinders blacker and denser since that morning of May 8th. The people all about the mountain and in the city, which was in its festival dress, were growing momentarily more and more anxious. Suddenly at 7:40 (as shown by the hospital clock, which stopped precisely at that instant and which alone has remained providentially standing above the ruins, as if to mark through all history the second at which the justice of God had struck) a tremendous detonation shook the whole colony, and an enormous mass was seen to mount with vertiginous rapidity straight into the air from the mouth of the crater. The black spirals of the column, shot through with electrical charges, unfolded, rolled off into space, and, driven by an invisible power, went afar to throw off the incandescent matter contained in their flanks. A spout-like column of flame meanwhile had abruptly disengaged itself from these great masses and had burst over St. Pierre like a hurricane, enveloping city, road-

125

stead, and suburbs in one dreadful net. It extended from the promontory of Carbet to the Morne Folic near Le Precheur, describing in the country round about the city a regular curve of from two to three kilometers. Nothing would convey an impression of the atmospheric disturbance produced by this fiery hurricane.

What did it contain? Matter in fusion? Burning gases or vapors? All these things together? God knows. "Everything went down before it," said to me a witness who was in a good position to see, "everything went down, and everything caught fire." Deep night spread over the land, but it was immediately illumined by the flames of this inferno. From the grass of the savannas to the produce of the fields, from the houses and edifices of the city to the ships in the roadstead, everywhere, on sea and land alike, there is but one great conflagration consuming 30,000 lives.

While the fiery tornado, passing southward and westward, widened the sweep of its destructive power in order to extend its devastations farther, another remarkable phenomenon came to stop it in its course. Two strong atmospheric currents, laden with rain, moving, one from the southeast, the other from the north, fell of a sudden upon the sides of the fiery spout, and, encircling it along a distinctly marked line, cooled it to such a point that I have seen persons who, finding themselves precisely upon this line of demarcation, were struck on one side by fiery missiles, while on the other and only a few feet away nothing was falling but the rain of mud, cinders, and stones which descended on the countryside everywhere.

FRIDAY, May 9: According to the statistics of the parishes of St. Pierre, contained in the ordo of the diocese, the city comprised somewhat more than 27,000 souls. Add to this number perhaps 2,000 refugees who had fled into the town seeking safety and at least 500 sailors from the ships in the roadstead with 1,000 souls who succumbed to the scourge in the parishes of Carbet and Le Precheur, and we have a total exceeding 30,000. Taking into account, however, that for two or three days prior to the disaster many persons (and women in particular) had begun to leave St. Pierre, I think I am very close to the truth in placing the number of our dead at 30,000.

126

SATURDAY, May 10: The administration, civil and military is disorganized. Would one believe it? Preparations for the elections are going forward for tomorrow, at least in the arron-dissement of Fort-de-France*. That of St. Pierre has ceased to be. The hull of the American packet is still burning in the roadstead at St. Pierre. There rises from it a great stench of putrefaction. We disembark, provided with disinfectants, on the Place Bertin, once so full of life and movement. We pick our way through the wreck. The Place is now nothing but a heap of confused ruins. Here and there are decaying bodies, horribly disfigured, and showing by the contraction of the limbs how awful must have been the death-agony. Among the seared branches of a fallen tamarind tree, which proved in-adequate to protect him, we find the body of a poor creature lying on his back with his head raised and his arms stretched to heaven in a gesture of supplication . . . .

It is with difficulty that we could reach the cathedral, it being impossible to recognize the streets. In the interior of the houses (the walls of which are standing in places) there are still flaming and smoking braziers. Hot stones, iron, lime, cinders, materials of all sorts scorched the soles of our feet. It was im-prudent even to touch the charred walls, which crumble at the slightest shock.

One of the square cathedral towers with its four bells is still upright; but it is riddled throughout, and we dare not approach it. The left tower has been thrown down together with its great bell. The statue of the Virgin, belonging to the facade, seemed to me to be intact as it lay among the ruins in front of the Cathedral. The walls with the exception of the apse have dis-appeared. We made our way in through the Rue du College and saw several bodies in the ruins. Here as elsewhere most of the victims are buried under the piled-up masonry. . . .

I was in haste to leave this desolation. On returning to the Place Bertin I tried in vain to find the church of the Fort. The Seminaire-College is *tabula rasa.* I am told that in the center it

---

*It was this inane insular election that caused the governor of Martinique to act and die so senselessly and caused so many people to stay (or be forced to stay) in St. Pierre — a primary thesis of Thomas and Witts' book, *The Day the World Ended.*

is impossible to distinguish the spot where the church stood. This is the sum of our losses: your episcopal residence, your cathedral, all the churches of the city, that of Ste. Philomene and of Trois-Ponts, the parsonages, all the coffers of the factories and of the episcopate, the coffers of the ecclesiastical retired lists, etc.

The *Suchet's* mission, after it had recovered the treasury of the bank, was to help in the evacuation of Le Precheur. Two hundred inhabitants were taken aboard under a heavy shower of cinders from the volcano. Two small boats filled with women and children capsized under the ship. The sailors of the *Suchet* showed the finest courage and saved all souls.

MONDAY, May 19: The violence of the volcano appears to be increasing; and the clouds of cinders are falling everywhere over the colony. Today the party disembarked, but orders were immediately given to put to sea again. A mighty eruption has taken place. We live under ashes here at Fort-de-France, only 25 kilometers as the crows fly from the crater, and, I may add, in continual anxiety. . . .

Fort-de-France and the whole southern portion of the colony are filled with refugees. An effort has been made to distribute them among the various communes; but we still have more than 7,000 with us.

TUESDAY, May 20: Another date for Martinique . . . At 5:15, while I was dressing, I heard two of the loudest and most pro- longed volcanic explosions, I think, that have yet taken place. I called to Abbé Recourse, who has been sleeping in the room under mine since having given up his own house to a family of refugees. "The volcano is behaving badly," I said. "Something is going to happen." At the same instant I beheld above the peaks of Carbet toward Mont Pelée in the distance a rolling fire of lightning flashes, issuing from a black spot in the sky and accompanied by a deep rumbling of thunder. Thereupon the first spirals of the dread column began to mount upward from the black spot. I called to Abbé Recourse once more, "Come quickly."

We both looked on not without terror, as this strange meteor went up and still farther up, unfolding its convolutions, reaching incredible heights, then drawing nearer us, spreading out to all

points of the compass, filling the upper spaces, still rolling onward till it hung over our head, giving us the feeling that this
was the end of Martinique! What would come next? Were we
to perish under fire like St. Pierre or under ashes like Pompeii?

We were ready. We continued to watch the immense cloud,
reddened in the east by the rising sun. I had fallen on my knees,
awaiting God's hour, when a veil of vapors, like a curtain drawn
across a scene at the theater, completely closed off the aerial
column from our sight. And the town, just awaking?   A great
sound arose, and then everyone was fleeing for life. The church
was looked upon as a place of safety by many. The crowd
surged into it and up to the altar-steps . . . . Here were such
scenes as might take place if the end of the world had come.

A quarter of an hour of anguish passed thus. Then began the
rain of lava and cinders. When the first stones fell, I looked for
flames; but I was soon reassured. We were saved once more. We
had suffered naught but fright. We had incidentally collected a
fine assortment of volcanic stones, some of them the size of an
egg. Nearer the volcano others were found that were much
larger.

But what of the parishes closer to the mountain? The *Suchet*
left at once on its reconnoitering expedition. The news it
brought back was that the phenomenon which had annihilated
St. Pierre had recurred exactly under the same conditions. Whatever was left standing in the ill-fated city had been razed by the
second fire-spout. Not a stone of St. Pierre now stands upon
another. A few houses on the confines of the first scourge were
reached and demolished by the second. There are no new
victims.

WEDNESDAY, May 21: The consequences of this last day are
incalculable. All those who were beginning to regain a little
courage have sunk into profound despair. Thousands are taking
ship for St. Lucia, Guadeloupe, Trinidad, France, and the United
States. This is not only the exodus of the north toward the
south but of the whole of Martinique toward the outside world.

Here then, Monseigneur, is the life that we are leading. However it may be, since Providence has chosen that I should witness such events, I can only follow the example of Père Mary
and of our other colleagues. I shall be the last to abandon
Martinique.

129

AT THE CITY OF ST. PIERRE TODAY
WHAT IS TO BE SEEN

On the site of St. Pierre today there are many gaping ruins with trees growing between the roofless walls. Though the town has been partially resettled, it has never again regained its vivacity. Overlooking the bay is a small white building with a pillared entrance. It is a museum built and maintained largely by American citizens; there are many mementos of the great eruption of 1902 as well as of other volcanic explosions all over the world. The curator is an aged Martiniquais named Joseph Bonnet-Durival, who was living just outside St. Pierre on that terrible May morning in 1902.

A RECOLLECTION BY A STILL LIVING EYE-WITNESS OF 1902 – JOSEPH BONNET-DURIVAL, CURATOR OF THE LOCAL MUSEUM

"I was at the very landmark where stopped the eruption between St. Pierre and the next village, Carbet. In the next cottage our neighbors were killed, we not. We ran away, but by fear, because there was no time to lose: in half a minute the town was destroyed. It was an explosion. The eruption was a cloud of water steam carrying stones and ashes with a heat of 1000°C. and rolling along the ground with a speed of 500 feet per second (our volcano had made the atomic bomb before the scientists). Then I saw very well the eruption coming down to St. Pierre and towards us with a dreadful noise of boiling water. The cloud, running on the ground, had passed at some distance from us, but from its edge over us we received little hot pieces of coal, stones, and much water from its condensation. . . They arrived on us burning, but not too much. Running to the other village, we were stoned hard, wet and with cement on us (the water and ashes forming a paste). The eruption was over, but while running we were afraid, seeing the houses burning behind us in the country with high flames – not ours, because by the best blessing it was the first cottage safe towards the south. In the evening, when I was going to Fort de France by sea from the other village, Carbet, I saw in the harbor of St. Pierre the liner *Roraima* still burning with a high flame at 6 P.M., ten hours after the eruption, which had taken place about 8 o'clock in the morning. You could never forget those events."

In L. Thomas' article, "Prelude to Doomsday," in *American Heritage,* August 1961

THE CATASTROPHE
IN ST VINCENT

A NEARBY DISASTER

Had it not been for the annihilation of St. Pierre, the disaster at St. Vincent, British West Indies, a day earlier would have dominated the world's headlines. Thus the deaths of some 2000 St. Vincentians and the vast eruption of La Soufrière (one of several craters in the West Indies thus named) on May 7, 1902, were overshadowed in the public mind. The eruption's arrival was not unheralded. A few weeks before shocks had from time to time been felt on the island, more acutely on the leeward side in the vicinity of the crater. On May 6th La Soufrière had given out great clouds of vapor as well as an outpouring of ashes. Observers reported that the crown of the volcano seemed to be a ring of fire. At 3 P.M. there was an explosion.

But the great paroxysm took place the day following. Vast discharges of ash, bombs, boulders, and what probably was a black atomic dust poured from the trembling cone. There were many explosions. Floods of lava and mud poured down the major river beds, and the whole valley of the Walliabou River was said to resemble a chain of crater belching steam. At 8 A.M., the same time St. Pierre perished, La Soufrière began pouring its molten contents to the eastward, down the valley of the Rabacca River, wiping out completely the town of Rabacca. So dense were the clouds and so black the gloom that residents of the capital, Georgetown, fled for safety to the south.

It is difficult even to imagine the awesome spectacle of simultaneous eruptions of fire over both Pelée and Soufrière, though La Soufrière had erupted in 1718, 1785 and 1812. As a natural phenomenon, the Soufrière eruption was far greater, fiercer, and more terrific since the territory it devastated was far wider (one third of the island) and its natural changes more astonishing, unlike the terrifying results of Pelée. As there had been in Martinique, so there was talk of abandoning St. Vincent but slowly the colony recovered. Yet La Soufrière serves as a reminder, and the Rabacca is yet dry. Below are given once again the headlines (where they were to be seen) and one eye witness account from the several in *The Century Magazine* for August 1902 given to S. C. Reid of the USS *Dixie,* seen already .

NOTES ON THE PRELIMINARY ERUPTION
BY HERR MATHES

TUESDAY, May 6, 1902.

2:40 P.M.: First appearance of a white stream in consequence of a noise like a gunshot.

4:00 P.M.: The first people arrived at Chateaubelair who had fled from Richmond.

4:30 P.M.: People arrived from Morne Ronde.

5:15 P.M. I saw the reflection of fire on the steam cloud quite distinctly.

5:20 P.M. Very thick smoke arising from the foot of Soufrière on the right side, seen from Chateaubelair — a new crater?

5:20 P.M. Reflection of fire in the old crater and now for the first time to be seen issue of smoke, probably from the new crater on top of the mountain.

5:40 P.M. The smoke and steam clouds disappear and leave the summit clear and clean.

6:05 P.M. New eruption with very thick smoke.

SOME HEADLINES ON THE ST. VINCENT AFFAIR

I. *The New York Times* Saturday 10 May 1902
    ERUPTION BEGINS FEAR FOR OTHER ISLANDS
    IT IS BELIEVED DOMINICA AND ST. VINCENT
    HAVE SUFFERED SEVERELY VOLCANO IN LATTER
    ISLAND ACTIVE

The New York Times Sunday 11 May 1902
ERUPTION BEGINS ON ST. VINCENT GREAT DEVAS-
TATION WROUGHT ON ISLAND 30 DEATHS RE-
PORTED THE VOLCANO LA SOUFRIÈRE HAD BEEN
ACTIVE 9 DAYS ASHES WERE TWO FEET THICK
DOWNFALL OF DUST VERY HEAVY IN BARBADOS
LOUD REPORT RESEMBLING ARTILLERY HEARD
ON THAT ISLAND

The New York Times Monday 12 May 1902
HUNDREDS DEAD IN ST. VINCENT IT IS BELIEVED
THAT ABOUT 500 HAVE PERISHED VOLCANO STILL
ACTIVE SEVERAL DISTRICTS DESTROYED HAVOC
WROUGHT UNKNOWN A FAMINE IS NOW THREAT-
ENED TWO BRITISH WARSHIPS CARRY SUPPLIES
FOR THE SUFFERERS COLUMNS OF VAPOR FROM
LA SOUFRIÈRE RISE 8 MILES HIGH

II. *The Boston Globe* Friday 9 May 1902
ALARM IN ST. VINCENT SOUFRIERE VOLCANO IN
THAT ISLAND CONTINUES IN ACTIVITY INHABI-
TANTS NEAR IT FLEEING DOMINICA AND ST.
VINCENT ARE FEARED TO HAVE SUFFERED
SEVERELY CABLES TO GRENADA AND ST. VIN-
CENT NOT WORKING

The Boston Globe Saturday 10 May 1902
ST. VINCENT NOW DUST AN INCH THICK AT
BRIDGETOWN BARBADOS 100 MILES FROM LA
SOUFRIÈRE ST. VINCENT'S VOLCANO TREMEN-
DOUS ERUPTION YESTERDAY OF VOLCANO
SOUFRIÈRE AT ST. VINCENT BRITISH WEST INDIES

The Boston Globe Sunday 11 May 1902
ERUPTION AT ST. VINCENT SOUND LIKE ARTIL-
LERY HEARD 100 MILES AWAY AT BARBADOS,
WHICH IS COVERED WITH SEVERAL INCHES OF
DUST

The Boston Globe Monday 12 May 1902
HORRORS INCREASED VOLCANIC OUTBREAK ON
ST. VINCENT WITH GREAT DEATH SWEEP ST. VIN-
CENT IN DARKNESS DENSE BLACK FOG CINDERS
AND SAND MAKE ISLAND INVISIBLE TO ST. LUCIA

III. *The Boston Post* Sunday 11 May 1902
ISLAND OF ST. VINCENT LAID WASTE VOLCANIC
ACTIVITY IN DOMINICA ST. VINCENT ISLAND
COVERED WITH ASHES ERUPTION CONTINUES

THE NATIONAL GEOGRAPHIC
ON THE ERUPTION OF MT. PELÉE

The National Geographic Society with the blessings of President Theodore Roosevelt sent a scientific expedition (one of the Society's first) to Martinique and St. Vincent to report on the eruptions that had occurred on these West Indian Islands in May 1902 almost simultaneously. In the June issue there were articles (from which we have drawn for this booklet), but readers were compelled to wait until July when members of the Expedition filed their illustrated reports on the events. These articles' titles are listed below. Brief notices on Mt. Pelée appeared again in the *National Geographic Magazine* for December 1902, November 1903, and December 1906.

June 1902:   "The NGS Expedition to Martinique and St. Vincent", pp. 183-4 — mere note of formation and exodus
"Volcanoes", pp. 204-8 — the basics on this subject
"Magnetic Disturbances Caused by the Explosion of Mt. Pelée", pp. 208-9
"NGS Expedition in the West Indies", pp. 209-19 — a brief chronicle of the doings

July 1902:   "Report on the Volcanic Disturbances in the West Indies," pp. 223-67 — THE report on St. Pierre
"The Recent Volcanic Eruption in the West Indies," pp. 268-85 — THE report on the St. Vincent eruption
"The Volcanic Rocks of Martinique and St. Vincent," pp. 285-96
"Chemical Discussion of Analyses of Volcanic Ejecta from Martinique & St. Vincent," pp. 296-99
"Reports of Vessels as to the Range of the Volcanic Dust," pp. 299-301

THE INDEX TO THE ERUPTION'S COVERAGE IN
THE NEW YORK TIMES
"THE DIARY OF THE WORLD"

† Numbers after date show page and column numbers.

* Another member of the National Geographic West Indies Expedition.

BIBLIOGRAPHY

The *Corpus Inscriptionum Latinarum:*

Volume IV, *Inscriptiones Parietariae Pompeianae, Herculanenses, Stabianae,* edited variously, 1871 ff., Berlin.

Volume IV, Supplement I, *Tabulae Ceratae Pompeiis Repertae,* ed. C. Zangemeister, 1898, Berlin.

Volume X, *Inscriptiones Campaniae,* ed. T. Mommsen, Berlin, 1883.

Books on the Texts:

Krenkel, W., *Pompeianische Inschriften,* Heidelberg, 1960
Geist, H., *Pompeianische Wandinschriften,* Munich, 1960
Onorato, G., *Iscrizioni Pompeiane,* Florence, 1965
Cole, H. W., *The Writing on the Wall,* New York, 1931
Lindsay, Jack, *The Writing on the Wall,* London, 1960

General Studies on Pompeii:

Mau, A., *Pompeii,* trans. F. W. Kelsey, New York, 1907
MacKendrick, P., *The Mute Stones Speak,* New York, 1960, Chap. VIII, "The Silent City".
Maiuri, A., *Pompeii,* Libreria dello Stato, Roma, 1954
_____ ., *Pompeii,* Istituto Geographico, Novara, 1960

General Studies on Herculaneum:

Barker, E. R., *Buried Herculaneum,* London, 1908
Deiss, J. J., *Herculaneum,* New York, 1966
Maiuri, A., *Herculaneum,* Libreria dello Stato, Roma, 1960

Outside the walls:

Seymour,   "Agriculture in the Life of Pompeii", *Y.C. Studies* IV, 165 ff, New Haven
Heron de Villefosse, A.M., *L'argenterie et les Bijoux d'or du Trésor de de Boscoreale,* Paris, 1903

BIBLIOGRAPHY

The *CORPVS INSCRIPTIONVM LATINARVM:*

VOLUME IV: *Inscriptiones Parietarias Pompeianas, Herculanenses, et Stabianas consilio et auctoritate Academiae Litterarum Regiae Borussicae* edidit Carolus Zangemeister

Accedunt Vasorum Fictilium ex eisdem oppidis erutorum Inscriptiones, editae a Riccardo Schoene

Adiectae sunt Tabulae Lithographae Quinquaginta Septem, Berolini, MDCCCLXXXI

VOLUME IV^2: *Inscriptionum Parietariarum Pompeianarum Supplementum* ediderunt Augustus Mau et Carolus Zangemeister

Accedunt Tabulae Ceratae, editae a Carolo Zangemeister et *Vasorum Fictilium Inscriptiones,* editae ab Augusto Mau

Pars I: *Tabulae Ceratae Pompeis repertae annis MDCCCLXXXV et MDCCCLXXXVII,* editae a Carolo Zangemeister, Berolini, MDCCCXCVIII

Pars II: *Inscriptiones Parietariae et Vasorum Fictilium,* editae ab Augusto Mau

Adiectae sunt Tabulae Lithographicae Tres et Forma Partis Pompeiorum Effossae, Berolini, MCMIX

Inscriptiones post absolutum volumen IV detactae

VOLUME IV^3: *Inscriptiones post absolutum alterum supplementum voluminis IV detectae*

Partes I-III: *Voluminis Quarti Supplementi Pars Tertia:* edidit Matthaeus Della Corte Inscriptiones Pompeianas Parietarias et Vasorum Fictilium, Berolini, MCMLII, MCMLV, MCMLXIII

Pars IV: *Inscriptiones Pompeianae Parietariae et Vasorum Fictilium annis 1951-1956 repertae:* edendas cruavit Fulcherus Weber

Inscriptiones Herculanenses Parietarias et Vasorum Fictilium edidit Pius Ciprotti, Berolini, MCMLXX

*VOLUME X: *Inscriptiones Bruttiorum, Lucaniae, Campaniae, Siciliae, et Sardiniae consilio et auctoritate Academiae Litterarum Regiae Borussicae* edidit Theodorus Mommsen, Berolini, MDCCCLXXXIII

Instrumentum Domesticum Regionum Italiae Primae et Tertiae edidit Theodorus Momsen, Berolini, MDCCCLXXXIII

*All numbers from this volume have been underlined in the text.

VOCABULARY

The words herein represent as completely as possible all the
Latin words in the text. Only personal names have been exclu-
ded, while geographic items are given with some documentation.
In addition for the convenience of the reader the following ab-
breviations have been employed: abl. = ablative, acc. = accusative, adv. = adverb, c. = common (both sexes), comp. = compara-
tive, conj. = conjunction, dat. = dative, defect. = defective, f. =
feminine, gen. = genitive, imper. = impersonal, indecl. = indeclinable, indef. = indefinite, inter. = interrogative, interj. = inter-
jection, irreg. = irregular, m. = masculine, n. = neuter, part, =
participle, pers. = personal, pl. = plural, post. = postpositive,
prep. = preposition, pron. = pronoun, reflex. = reflexive, semidep.
= smideponent, subj. = subjunctive.

A

a (prep. + abl.) from, by

ab prep. + abl) from, by

abeo, -ire, -ivi, -turus go (away)

aberro (1) wander away, digress

abicio, -ere, -ieci, -iectus throw
down, hurl

abluo, -ere, -ui, -utus wash,
clean

absens (-sentis) absent

ac (conj.) and

accipio, -ere, -cepi, -ceptus
receive

accubo, -ere, -cubui, -cubitus lie
down

accuratus, -a, -um full, exact

acroma, -atis, n. actor

actuarius, -i, m. registrar

actum, -i, n. deed, business

acer, acris, acre sharp, shrill

acetum, -i, n. vinegar

ad (prep. + acc.) to

addendus, -a, -um to be added

addo, -ere, -didi, -ditus add...to
apply, attack, quicken

adduco, -ere, -duxi, -ductus
lead on

adhuc (adv.) thus far

adicio, -iere, -ieci, -iectus throw
at, add

aditus, -us, m. entrance

adlego, -ere, -legi, -lectus
coopt, elect...to

admirabilis, -e worthy, to be ad-
mired, wonderful

admiratio, -ionis, f. amazement,
wonder

admiror (1) wonder at, admire

adulescens, -entis, m. young man

adversus (prep. + acc.) against

aedes, -is f. temple; in plur.
house

aedicuia, -ae, f. small chapel,
shrine

aedificum, -i, n. building

aedifico (1) build

aedilis, -is m. aedile, commissioner (the public official on
the bottom of the political
ladder in charge of the public
works in a city)

aedituus, -i, m. temple-keeper,
priest

aegroto (1) be sick

aeneus, -a, -um of bronze (or
brass)

aeque (adv.) equally

aerarium, -i, n. treasury (where
the *aes* is kept)

aes, aeris, n. bronze, money
aeternus, -a, -um eternal, ever-
lasting
Aethiopes, -um m. pl. blackmen
adfero, -ferre, -tuli, -latus bring
affigo, -ere, -fixi, -fixus fasten
afui - perf. of *absum,* be gone
ager, agri, m. field, depth
ago, -ere, egi, actus do, drive
force, celebrate, live
aio, ais, ait, aiunt (irreg.) say
(with direct quotation only)
albus, -a, -um white
alea, -ae, f. die, dice-game,
gambling
aliarus, -i, m. garlic-dealer
aliquis, aliqua, aliquid any
aliquot. (indecl.) several
alius, alia, aliud (an) other; alii...
alii, some...others; aliud...
aliud one thing...another
thing
allatus, -a, -um − from *adfero,*
bring
alligo (1) bind up, restrain
alphabetum, -i n. alphabet
altare, -is n. altar
alter, altera, alterum other (of
two)
altus, -a, -um high, deep
amabiliter (adv.) lovingly
amans, amantis, c. lover
ambustus, -a, -um scorched
amicio, -cere, -icui, -ictus throw
around, wrap
amicus, -i m. friend
amo (1) love, like
amor, amoris, m. love, darling
amphitheatrum, -i, n. amphitheatre (an elliptical building
for all sorts of fights)
amphora, -ae, f. a clay vessel
(with 2 handles), pitcher,
flask, jar bottle
amplexus, -a, -um − part of
amplector, embrace, carress
amplitudo, -dinis, f. size
ancilla, -ae, f. maid-servant,
female slave
angulus, -i, m. corner

anima, -ae, f. life, soul, darling
animadverto, -ere, -verti, -versus
notice
animal, -alis, n. living thing,
animal
animula, -ae, f. little soul, darling, life
animus, -i, mind, spirit, courage
annus, -i, m. year
ante (prep. + acc.) before, in
front of
antiquior (antiquioris) older
anulus, -i, m. ring
apes, apis, f. bee
aptatus, -a, -um fitted, equipped
appareo, -ere, -parui appear, become visible
appello (1) draw near to,
approach (+ dat.)
Aprilis, -e of April (the month
named after the verb *aperio*)
aqua, -ae, f. water
ara, -ae, f. altar
arca, -ae, f. chest box
architectus, -i, m. architect,
deviser
ardeo, -ere, arsi be on fire, burn
area, -ae, f. courtyard
argenteus, -a, -um of silver
argentum, -i, n. silver
aries, arietis, m. ram
arma, -orum, n. pl. arms, weapons
armarium, -i, n. cupboard, chest
articulus, -i, m. limb, joint
as, assis, m. the as (a little
Roman copper coin, our
"penny" or the English "far-
thing")
ascendo, -ere, ascendi, ascensus
climb up, mount
asellus, -i, m. donkey
aspicio, -ere, aspexi, aspectus
look at, behold, observe
asser, -eris, m. beam, pole, stake
assiduus, -a, -um persistent, in-
cessant
assurp, -ere, -surrexi, -surrectus
rise
ater, atra, atrum black
athleta, -ae, f. athletic context

Atila, -ae, f. a town in the vincinity of Pompeii (see map)
atque (conj.) and
atramentum, -i, n. ink, black liquid
atriensis, -is, m. majordomo
Atticus, -a, -um of Attica (the deme in which Athens is located)
attuli – from *adfero*, bring
auctio, -ionis, f. increase, auction
auctoritas, -tatis, f. authority, power
audio (4) hear, listen to
aufero, -ferre, abtuli, ablatus take away, destroy
augur, -uris, m. seer, interpreter, augur (a member of a priestly college who foretold the future by natural events or animal entrails)
Augustalis, -is, m. priest of Augustus (the first such group having been formed in Rome by the Emperor Tiberius)
Augustus, -i, m. the month of August (named after the first Emperor)
aura, -ae, f. breeze, wind
aureus, -a, -um of gold, golden
aureus, -i, m. gold coin
aurifex, -ficis, m. goldsmith
aus, auris, m. ear
aut (conj.) or; aut...aut, either...or
autem (adv.) however
auxilium, -i, n. help, aid
ave (interj.) hail! greetings!
avitus, -a, -um grandfather's, ancestral
avunculus, -i, m. uncle

B
babae (interj.) wonderful! strange!
babacculus, -i, m. poor fool
Badianus, -a, -um of Badia (a town in Spain, the modern Santa Maria de Bedoza)

beatitudo, -dinis f. happiness
bal(i) neum, -i, n. bath, bathhouse
barbarus, -i, m. barbarian, savage man
barba, -ae f. beard
basilica, -ae, f. basilica (a building with a double colonnade used for courts and exchange; adopted as a form of architecture by the Christian Church)
basio (1) kiss
bellum, -i n. war
bellus, -a, -um fine, handsome
bene (adv.) well
beneficium, -i, n. kindness
benemerens (benemerentis) well deserving
bibo, -ere, bibi, potus drink
bilychnis, -e double-lamped
bimus, -a, -um two years old
bini, -ae, -a a pair, two each
bis (adv.) twice
bisaceium, -i, n. saddle-bay
bisellium, -i, n. double seat, seat of honor (usually richly decorated)
blanditiae, -arum, f. pl. charms
blandus, -a, -um seductive
boletus, -i, m. mushroom
bonus, -a, -um good, fine
bos, bovis, c. cow, ox
brevis, -e short, brief
bulla, -ae, f. knob
bullatus, -a, -um wearing an amulet
buxiarius, -a, -um beech wood

C
cacator, -oris, m. befouler, defiler
caco (1) deficate
cado, -ere, cecidi, casurus fall, happen
caduceum, -i, m. ceiling
caelator, -oris, m. engraver
calamitas, -tatis, f. loss, harm, mishap
calamus, -i, m. reed-pen

caleo, -ere, calui be hot, glow

calidus, -a, -um warm, hot

caligo, -ginis, f. mist, fog, darkness

calix, calicis, m. cup, wine, pot

Campani, -orum, m. pl. Campanians
Campanians

Campania, -ae, f. Campania (the
district of Italy S. of Latium,
of which Naples is the chief
city)

Campanienses, -um, m. pl. the
people of Campania

Campanius, -a, -um of Campania,
Campagian

campus, -i, m. plain, field

candidus, -a, -um white, clear,
bright

canis, -is, c. dog

cano, -ere, cecini sing (of), pro-
claim

capillatus, -a, -um with (long)
hair

capio, -ere, cepi, captus take, seize

Capitaolium, -i, n. the Capitoline
(the chief of the 7 hills of
Rome and the political nerve
center)

Capua, -ae, f. Capua (the chief
city of Campania in ancient
times, the modern Sta. Maria
di Capua)

caput, capitis, n. head

caro, carnis, f. flesh, meat

carus, -a, -um dear, previous, be-
loved

caseus, -i, m. cheese

castra, -orum, n. pl. camp

castus, -a, -um pure, genuine,
100%

casula, -ae, f. little cottage

casus, -us, m. accident, chance,
(mis)fortune

catella, -ae, f. puppy

catena, -ae, f. chain, fetter

catenatio, -ionis, f. clamp, pin

caupona, -ae, f. cafe

causā (post. prep. + gen') for-
the-sake-of

causa, -ae, f. cause, case, reason

cavea, -ae, f. stall, cage, pen

caveo, -ere, cavi, cautus beware,
guard against, take care of

cavo (1) hollow out, erode

cecidi — perf. of cado, fall

cedo (interj.) come on!

cella, -ae, f. room

cena, -ae, f. dinner

cenaculum, -i, n. dining-room,
upper story

cenatio, -ionis, f. dining-room

ceno (1) dine, eat

censeo, -ere, censui, census
count, vote, decree

censio, -ionis, f. idea, motion,
vote

censor, -oris, m. censor (the title
of two elderly magistrates
sho presided over the census
and who punished moral or
political misdemeanors)

centiens (adv.) a hundred times

centum (indecl.) one hundred

ceratus, -a, -um covered with
wax

cerasinus, -a, -um cherry-colored

Ceres, Cereis, f. Ceres (goddess
of agriculture who figures
prominently in the nythology
of Sicily)

certe (adv.) indeed, certainly

certus, -a, -um certain, sure

cervical, -alis, n. pillow, cushion

cervix, -vicis, f. neck

cesso (1) cease, hesitate

ceteri, -ae, -a the rest, the remaining

ceterum (adv.) but

chalcidicium, -i, n. signature

chorus, -i, m. dance, chorus,
choir

cicer, -eris, m. pea

cinaedus, -i, m. sodomite,
"fairy", fop, fag

cingulum, -i, n. belt, leash

cinis, cineris, m. ash

circa (prep. + acc.) about,
around

circumfero, -ferre, -tuli, -latus
carry around

cisiarius, -i, m. carriage-driver
cithara, -ae, f. lyre, lute
cito (adv.) quickly
citra (prep. + acc.) on-this-side-of
citus, -a, -um quick, rapid
civitas, -tatis, f. state, city, citizenship
clamo (1) shout
clamor, -oris, m. shout(ing)
clarus, -a, -um bright, famous, clear
classis, -is, f. fleet
clibanarius, -i, m. blacksmith, baker
cliens, -entis, m. client, vassal
Clodianus, -a, -um of Cnidus (a city on the coast of modern Turkey, renowned for its statue of Venus & wine)
coccineus, -a, -um scarlet-covered
coepi, -isse (defect.) begin
coero (1) — a variant for curo, see to it
cognosco, -ere, -novi, -nitus make known, learn
cogo, -ere, coegi, coactus force, compel
coheres, -heredis, c. co-heir
colaphus, -i, m. blow
collapsus, -a, -um — from collabor, fall into ruins, collapse
collatus, -a, -um — from confero, bring together, collect
collega, -ae, m. colleague, associate
colligo, -ere, -lexi, -lectus collect, gather together
collis, -is, m. hill
colloco (1) establish, arrange, lay out
colo, -ere, colui, cultus worship, cultivate, dwell
colonia, -ae, f. abode, colony, town
colonus, -i, m. colonist, inhabitnat
columba, -ae, f. dove, pigeon
columbinus, -a, -um of a dove

columella, -ae, f. column, pillar
comedo, -ere, -edi eat up
comes, comitis, m. comrade, friend
commendo (1) entrust, commend
commisator, -oris, m. reveller
commiseror (1) bewail
commodo (1) oblige, supply, adopt
commodum, -i, n. convenience
commune, -is, n. community, commune
communis, -e common, public
comoedium, -i, n. comedy
complaudo, -ere, -plaudi, -plausus clap
complector, -plecti, -plexus embrace
componia, -ae, f. cookshop
conchyliatus, -a, -um dyed in purple
concido, -ere, -cidi fall (down)
concito (1) rouse
concupio, -pere, -piui, -pitus be very eager
condo, -ere, -didi, -ditus establish, hide, store
conductor, -oris, m. tenant, contractor
conficio, -ere, -feci, -fectus finish, accomplish
conicio, -cere, -cieci, -ciectus throw
coniunx, coniugis, c. spouse
conlapsus, -a, -um — from confero, bring together, collect
conor (1) try, attempt
conpareo, -ere, -parui appear
consecro (1) dedicate, consecrate
consensus, -us, m. agreement, general consent
consentio, -ire, -sensi, -sensus agree
conservo (1) save, preserve
considero (1) look at, examine
consilium, -i, n. plan, advice
consisto, -ere, stiti stop, halt
consolor (1) cheer, encourage

143

consono, -are, -sonui harmonize
conspicio, -ere, spexi, -spectus
   view, see
conspicuus, -a, -um visible, distinguished
constantia, -ae, f. courage
constituo, -ere, -stitui, -stitutus
   establish, decide
consul, -ulis, m. consul (the
   chief magistrate of Rome,
   after whom the year was
   named)
consulo, -ere, -sului, -sultus   look
   out for (+ dat.)
consulto (1) deliberate
consultum, -i, n. decree; with
   senatus, senatorial decree
consumo, -ere, -sumpsi, -sumptus
   spend, destroy, exhaust
contemno, -ere, -tempsi, -temp-
   tus slight, belittle, ignore
conterreo, -ere, -terrui, -territus
   terrify, hold
conticesco, -ere, -ticui become
   silent
contineo, -ere, -tinui, -tentus
   hold
contingit, -ere, -tigit it happens
continuus, -a, -um consecutive,
   unbroken, successive
contra (prep. + acc.) against
contuli – from *confero,* collect,
   match
contra (adv.) on the other hand
contrarius, -a, -um different,
   opposite
conubium, -i, n. rite of marriage
convenio, -ire, -veni, -ventus
   apply to, come together,
   convene
copiosus, -a, -um boundless, full
copus, -i, m. host, keeper of a
   wineshop
Corinthius, -a, -um of Corinthium
   ware
Cornelius, -a, -um of Cornelius
   (a renowned family including
   the Scipios and Gracchi,
   whose scion Sulla brought
   Pompeii into Roman control
   in 86 B.C. and whose name
   was given to the city)

cornicen, -cinis, m. horn-player
corona, -ae, f. wreath, crown
corpus, corporis, n. body
corripio, -ere, -ripui, -reptus
   seize, take away
corrotundo (1) round up
Corsicus, -a, -um of Corsica (the
   uppermost large island off
   Italy's west coast)
cos. – a most common abbreviation for *consulibus* in the "ablative of consulship"
Cous, -a, -um of Cos (an island
   in the Aegean Sea near the
   coast of modern Turkey, renowned for its wine, weaving,
   and Hippocrates, the father
   of medical arts)
craticula, -ae, f. little baskey
creber, crebra, crebrum
   frequent, thick
credo, -ere, credidi, creditus
   believe
credra, -ae, f. lemon
Cretensis, -is, c. a Cretan (an
   inhabitant of the isle of Crete)
Creticus, -a, -um of Crete (the
   island belonging to Greece,
   the seat of Minoan civiliza-
   tion)
crevi – from *cresco,* grow
crus, crucis, f. pole, cross, leg
crypta, -ae, f. covered gallery,
   subterranean passage
cubiculum, -i, n. bedroom
culcitra, -ae, f. pillow
culo (1) back up
cum (conj.) when, since, although
cum (prep. + acc.) with
Cumae, -arum, f. pl. Cumae
   (the first Greek settlement in
   Italy on the coast of Campania above Naples, renowned for its prophecying Sibyl,
   with many ruins still visible)
Cumanus, -a, -um of Cumae
cunctor (1) delay, hesitate
cunctus, -a, -um all, entire
cuneus, -i, m. wedge, row of
   seats

cupidus, -a, -um eager for
(+dat.)
cupio (4) desire, wish
cur (inter. part.) why?
cura, -ae, f. care, concern
curiosus, -a, -um careful, diligent
curo (1) take care, see to it
curro, -ere, -cucurri, cursurus run
cursus, -us, m. race, speed,
course
custodia, -ae, f. guarding, protection
custodio (4) guard, protect

D

de (prep. + abl.) from, concerning
debeo, -ere, debui, debitus
ought, owe
December, -ris, -re of December
(the 10th month of the old
Roman calendar)
decerno, -ere, decrevi, decretus
decree
decipio, -ere, cepi, -ceptus
cheat, beguile, lull
decresco, -ere, -crevi, cretus
grow less, wane
decretum, -i, n. resolution,
decree
decuria, -ae, f. judicial panel
decurio, -ionis, m. town coun-
cillor, councilman
dedicatio, -ionis, f. dedication
dedico (1) set apart for a deity,
dedicate
deduco, -ere, -duxi, -ductus
bring (down), lead (down),
take (away)
defensor, -oris, m. guardian,
protector
defero, -ferre, -tuli, -latus carry
(down), bring, grant, report
deficio, -ere, -feci, -fectus fail,
be exhausted, go into eclipse
defrutum, -i, n. boiled-down
must (unfermented wine)
dein (adv.) then, next
deinde (adv.) then, next
deleo, -ere, -levi, -letus wipe
out, destroy

demum (adv.) at last
denarius, -i, m. a denarius (the
usual Roman value of cur-
rency, worth about 5¢)
densus, -a, -um thick, crowded
deprehendo, -ere, -hendi, -hensus
seize, catch, perceive, detect
descendo, -ere, -scendi, -scensus
climb down, descend
describo, -ere, -scripsi, -scriptus
copy down
desertus, -a, -um unfrequented,
deserted
desidero (1) miss, need, long for
designatus, -a, -um elect
destituo, -ere, -tui, -tutus stop,
abandon
destrictarium, -i, n. rubdown
room
destruo, -ere, -truxi, -tructus
pull down
detergeo, -ere, -tersi, tersus wipe
deus, -i m. god
devoro (1) sulp down, devour,
waste
dexter, dextra, dextrum right,
favorable
diaria, -orum, n. pl. rations
dico, -ere, dixi, dictus say, tell
dicto (1) declare, remark
didici – from disco, learn
dies, diei, c. day
differo, -ferre, distuli, dilatus
scatter, separate, put off
diffundo, -ere, -fundi, -fusus
pour, spread, gladden
dignus, -a, -um worthy of, be-
fitting, fit for (+ abl.)
diligenter (adv.) with care
dimitto, -ere, -misi, -missus send
away, dismiss
dipudium, -i, n. the sum of 2
asses
discedo, -ere-cessi, -cessurus
depart, withdraw
discens, discentis, m. student
discumbo, -ere, -cubui,
cubiturus, take place at table
discursus, -us, m. running to and
fro, zigzaging

145

dispensatari, -aris, m. steward
distinguens (-entis) distinctive
diu (adv.) for a long time
diutius (adv.) longer
divido, -ere, -visi, -visus separate,
    divide, distribute
divus, -a, -um divine, deified (a
    title given to certain Roman
    emperors by the Senate after
    death)
do, date, dedi, datus give
dolium, -i, n. jar (a large type of
    globular form with a wide
    mouth)
dolor, -oris, m. grief
domina, -ae, f. mistress
dominicus, -a, -um the master's
dominus, -i, m. master
domitus, -a, -um – from domo,
    train, subdue
domus, -us f. house, home
donec (conj.) until
donum, -i, n. gift, present
dormio (4) sleep
dos, dotis, f. dowry, gift,
    property
dubius, -a, -um doubtful, inde-
    cisive
ducenti, -ae, -a two hundred
duco, -ere, duxi, dectus bring,
    lead, marry
dulcis, -e sweet, delightful,
    charming; with aqua, sweet
dum (conj.) while
dumtaxat (conj. + subj.) as long
    as, provided that
duo, duae, duo two
duodevicesimus, -a, -um
    eighteenth
duro (1) harden, toughen, en-
    dure
durus, -a, -um hard, tough,
    harsh
duumvir, -viri, m. mayor (with
    only a one year term)
dux, ducis, m.. general leader

E

eboreus, -a-um of ivory
ebrietas, -tatis, f. drunkeness

ecce (intarj.) lo! behold!
edendus, -a, -um to be given
edictum, -i, n. proclamation,
    edict, manifesto
effiuo, -ere run out
effringo, -ere, fregi, -fractus
    break open
effulgeo, -ere, -fulsi shine out,
    gleam
effundo, -ere, -fundi, -fusus pour
    forth
ego, mei, mihi, me (pron.) I
egredior, egredi, egressus go
    forth
eheu (interj.) alas!
elephantus, -i, m. elephant,
    ivory
embolum, -i, n. beak
emo, -ere, emi, emptus buy
emptio, -ionis, f. buying,
    purchase
emptus, -a, -um – from emo,
    buy
enim (poastpos. conj.) for
eo (adv.) there, to that place
eo, ire, ivi, iturus, go
epistula, -ae, f. letter
epulo, -onis, m. feaster; with
    septemvir, a priest (one of a
    college of priests, who super-
    intended the sacrificial ban-
    quets to the gods)
epulum, -i, n. banquet
equa, -ae, f. mare
equestris, -e equestrain, middle-
    class, nice
ergo (adv.) therfore
eripio, -ere, -ripui, -reptus
    remove, save; with se escape
erubesco, -ere, -rubui, turn red
eruditus, -a, -um learned, edu-
    cated
et (conj.) and; et...et, both...
    and
etaim (adv.) also, even
evado, -ere, -vasi, -vasurus
    escape, do away
everro, -ere, verri, -versus sweep
exaequo (1) make level, even
    out

146

exaro (1) plow up, raise, write, note

excandesco, -ere, -candui grow angry

excedo, -ere, -cessi, -cessurus go out

excellens (-entis) extra-fine

excelsus, -a, -um high, lofty

excerpo, -ere, cerpsi, cerptus pick out, choose

excido, -ere, -cidi, fall, slip

excito (1) call out, rouse, incite

exeo, -ire, -ivi, -iturus go out

exerceo, -ere, -cui, -citus train

exigo, -ere, -egi, -actus drive forth, move, finish, spend

experior, -iri, -pertus test, try

exprimo, -ere, -pressi, -pressus press, form

exspecto (1) wait for, expect

extendo, -ere, -tendi, -tensus stretch

exterior, exterius outer

extra (prep. + acc.) outside, beyond

extremus, -a, -um end of

F

faba, -ae, f. bean

Fabianus, -a, -um Fabius'

fabula, -ae, f. story tale

facio, -ere, feci, factus do, make

factum, -i, n. deed

faenum, -i, n. hay

Falernus, -a, -um Falernian (a district in northern Campania famous for its wine)

fallo, -ere, fefelli, falsus deceive, disappoint, cheat

falsus, -a, -um wrong, untrue

familia, -ae, f. family, group

familiaris, -e intimate

fasces, -ium, m. pl. fasces

fascia, -ae, f. breast-band

fastido (1) despise, scorn

fateor, fateri, fassus admit, acknowledge

faustus, -a, -um lucky, blessed, fortunate

faveo, -ere, favi, faustus favor, support (+ dat.)

favilla, -ae, f. cinder, ash

Februarius, -a, -um of February (the month named after Feber, goddess of Fever)

felicitas, -tatis, f. good health

feliciter (interj.) bravo, hurrah (for), good luck (to) (+ dat.)

felix (felicis) prosperous, fortunate

fellator, -oris, m. sucker

fello (1) suck

femina, -ae, f. woman

Feretrius, -i, m. a surname of Jupiter ("he who subdues enemies")

fere (adv.) almost, nearly

feritas, -tatis, f. savageness, ferocity

fermentum, -i, n. leaven, start

fero, ferre, tuli, latus bring

ferumino (1) glue, cement

ferveo, -ere boil, steam

fictilis, -e made of clay, earthen

fidelis, -e faithful, loyal

fides, ei, f. faith, credit

figo, -ere, fixi, fixus plant, attach

figura, -ae f. form, shape, figure

figulinus, -a, -um of a potter

filius, -i, m. son

fingo, -ere, finxi, fictus shape, arrange, pretend

finis, -is, c. end, limit

finio (4) end, finish

fio, fieri, factus to be done, become, be made

flamen, flaminis, m. a flamen (the priest of one particular imperial deity)

flamma, -ae, f. blaze, flame

flecto, -ere, flexi, flectus turn, bend

flos, floris, m. flower, blossom, essence

folium, -i, n. leaf

fons, fontis, m. spring, fountain, source

foras (adv.) outside, abroad

forma, -ae, form, shape

formidolosus, -a, -um alarming, terrible

147

fortis, -e brave, courageous,
  strong
fortitudo, -dinis, f. bravery,
  courage
forum, -i n. forum, marketplace
  (where public matters & business was transacted)
frango, -ere, fregi, fractus break,
  wreck, shatter
frater, fratris, m. brother
frequentia, -ae f. throng, mob
frigidus, -a, -um cold, chill, dull
frons, frontis, f. forehead, front,
  breath
frugi (indecl.) honest, upright
fuco, -are, futui, fututus have
  sexual intercourse with
fuga, -ae f. flight, escape
fugio, -ere, fugi, fugiturus flee
fulcio, -ire, fulsi, fultus prop up,
  support
fulcrum, -i, n. post, foot, couch
fullo, -onis, m. fuller, cleaner
fullonica, -ae, f. the fuller's
  craft, fulling, cleaning, cleaner's shop
fullonicus, -a, -um of a fuller
fultus, -a, -um — from *fulcio,*
  support
fumus, -i, m. smoke
fundamentum, -i, n. foundation,
  groundwork
Fundi, -orum, m. pl. a seacoast
  town in Latium between
  Formiae & Terracina on the
  Appain Way
fundus, -i, m. ground, bottom
  farm, (plow)land, estate
funus, funeris, n. burial, funeral
fur, furis, m. thief, knave
furfur, -uris, m. bran
furunculus, -i, m. petty thief,
  smalltime operator

G

gallinaceus, -a, -um of poultry
garum, -i, n. fish-sauce (made of
  salted fishguts and small fish)
gaudeo, -ere, gavisus (semidep.)
  be glad, rejoice
gaudium, -i, n. joy, delight

gemma, -ae, f. bud, jewel,
  signet ring
gemmarius, -i, m. jeweler
genius, -i, m. spirit, inborn
  virtue
gens, gentis, f. family, race
  lineage
genus, generis, n. kind, type
Germanicus, -i, m. victor over
  Germany
Germinanus, -a, -um Germinus'
gladiator, -oris, m. swordsman
gladiatorius, -a, -um of gladiators
glis, gliris, m. dormouse
gloria, -ae, f. fame, glory
Gortynaei, -orum, m. pl. the
  people of Gortyns (a city in
  northern Crete with extensive
  remains, especially the long-
  est known Greek inscription,
  a law code of the 6th century
  B.C.)
Gortyneum, -i, n. the city of
  Gortyns
gradus, -us, m. step, pace
Graeculus, -i, m. little Greek
grandis, -e large, great
granum, -i, n. seed
graphium, -i, n. stylus, pen
gratis (adv.) for nothing
gratus, -a, -um pleasing, pleasant
gravis, -e heavy, severe
gressus, -us, m. step, gait
grex, gregis, m. flock, herd,
  troop
gubernator, -oris, m. pilot
gustaticium, -i, n. antipasto,
  whetter of the appetite
gustatio, -ionis, f. appetizer
gusto (1) taste
gypsatus, -a, -um covered with
  plaster

H

HS — the standard abbreviation
  for *sestertius,* the ordinary
  Roman unit of accounting,
  worth 2½ asses or 5¢
habeo, -ere, habui, habitus have,
  hold
habito (1) live, dwell
habitus, -us, m. state, condition

148

hactenus (adv.) thus far, hitherto
hallex, hallicis, f. sediment of
fish-sauce, garum
harena, -ae, f. sand, shore
haurio, -ire, hausi, haustus
drink, drain
(h)ave (interj.) hail! greetings!
Herculanenses, -ium, m. pl. the
people of Herculaneum
Herculanensis, -e of Herculaneum
Herculaneum, -i, n. another
major town buried by Vesuvius in 79 AD, now called
Erculano
Herculeus, -a, -um of Hercules
(patron & legendary founder
of Herculaneum)
heres, heredis, m. heir
heri (adv.) yesterday
hīc (adv.) here, in this place
hic, haec, hoc this
hilaris, -e cheerful, merry
hinc (adv.) hence, then
Hispania, -ae, f. Spain
historia, -ae, f. history, inquiry
homo, hominis, m. man, human
being
homuncio, -ionis, m. poor man
honestus, -a, -um honest, real,
genuine
honor, -oris, m. public office
honor; with causā, honorary
honorarius, -a, -um honorary
hora, -ae, f. hour
horologium, -i, n. clock, sundial
horreo, -ere, horrui shudder,
dread
horreum, -i, n. barn
horribilis, -e, dreadful, horrible
hortor (1) encourage, urge
hortus, -i, m. garden
hospes, hospitis, m. guest, host
hospitium, -i, n. lodging, inn,
hotel
hostis, -is, m. enemy
huc (adv.) here, to this place

I

iaceo, -ere, -iacui lie (dead)
iactura, -ae, f. loss

iam (adv.) now
ianua, -ae, f. door
Ianuarius, -a, -um of January
(the month named after the
double-faced god Janus)
ibi (adv.) there, in that place
idem (adv.) likewise
idem, eadem, idem the same
ideo (adv.) therfore
idoneus, -a, -um suitable
Idus, -uum, f. pl. the Ides (the
15th of all months but March
July, October, & May)
igitur (adv.) therefore
ignis, -is, m. fire
ignotus, -a, -um uncertain
Ilias, -adis, f. Homer's *Iliad*
ille, illa, illud that
illic (adv.) there, in that place
illuc (adv.) there, to that place
imago, -ginis, c. picture
imminens (-entis) overhanging,
threatening
immineo, -ere, -minui threaten
(+ dat.)
imperator, -oris, m. commander-
in-chief; when capitalized,
Emperor
impono, -ere, -posui, positus
put on, place on
imprudentia, -ae, f. foolishness
imus, -a, -um lowest, bottom of
in (prep. + abl.) in, during
in (prep. + acc.) into, toward
incendium, -i, n. fire, conflagration
incertus, -a, -um unsure,
uncertain
incido, -ere, -cidi, -casurus fall
(upon), happen, occur
incipio, -ere, -cepi, -ceptus begin
incola, -ae, m. inhabitant,
dweller
incommodus, -a, -um trouble-
some
incresco, -ere, -crevi increase
indecens (-entis) unseemly, un-
sightly
indico (1) declare, point out
indigens (-entis) poor, ready
infans, -antis, c. infant, baby

infelix (-felicis) unfruitful, unhappy, unlucky

infra (prep. + acc.) under, below

infero, -ferre, -tuli, -latus introduce

ingens (-ntis) huge

ingenuus, -a, -um freeborn, native, inborn

inimicus, -i, m. personal enemy

iniuria, -ae, f. insult, damage

innitor, -niti, -nixus leap on, rest on

inquam (defect.) say (always placed after one or more words of a direct quotation)

inquietus, -a, -um restless

inscribo, -ere, -scripsi, -scriptus inscribe

inscriptio, -ionis, f. title, inscription

insequor, -sequi, -secutus follow after

inspicio, -cere, -spexi, -spectus look at

insula, -ae, f. island, apartment house

integer, intergra, integrum whole, fresh

intentus, -a, -um strained, tense, intent, absorbed

inter (prep. + acc.) among, between

interdum (adv.) now and then, at times

interficio, -ere, -feci, -fectus kill

interpello (1) interrupt

interpretor (1) interpret, prophecy

interrogatio, -ionis, f.. investigation, examination

interrogo (1) ask

intoneo, -are, -tonui thunder

intra (prep. + acc.) within, inside

intro (adv.) within, inside

inusitatus, -a, -um unusual, strange

invenio, -ere, -veni, -ventus find, discover

invictus, -a, -um unbeaten, unconquered

invideo, -ere, -vidi, -visus begrudge

invidiosus, -a, -um jealous, spiteful

invulneratus, -a, -um unwounded

io (interj.) oh! hurrah!

ipse, ipsa, ipsum very, -self

irrumo (1) abuse, deceive, give suck

irrumpo, -ere, -rupi, -ruptus break in, rush in

ira, -ae, f. anger

iratus, -a, -um angry, enraged

is, ea, id that, this; he, she, it

Isiacus, -i, m. follower if Isis

Isis, Isdis, f. Isis (an Egyptian goddess, whose cult was widely exported from its homeland in the 1st century B.C.)

Italia, -ae, f. Italy (the boot-shaped country of southern Europe named after Italus, a native king)

Itaque (adv.) and so

iterum (adv.) again, for the second time

iubeo, -ere, iussi, iussus order

iudex, iudicis, m. judge

iugum, -i, n. yoke, mountain-ridge

Iulius, -a, -um of July (the month named after Julius Caesar, a reformer of the calendar by his own order)

Iunius, -a, -um of June (the month named after Juno, queen of the gods)

Iuppiter, Iovis, m. Jupiter (chief of the Roman gods)

iurgium, -i, n. insult

ius, iuris, n. right, jurisdiction; with *dicundo,* with judicial power

iussus, -us, m. order, command

iuvenis, -is, c.. young man, youth (between the ages of 20 and 45)

iuvo, -are, iuvi, iutus help, aid

K

Kalendae, -arum, f. pl. the Kalends (the first of each month)

L

Labyrinthus, -i, m. labyrinth (the name of the palace addition built by Daedalus for Kinos Minos of Crete; usually identified as part of the Palace of Knossos)

Lacedaemon, -monis, m. the ancient city of Sparta on the southern isle of Greece, the Peloponnese

laconicum, -i, n. sweating-room (first devised by the Spartans who lived in the area of Greece also called Laconia)

lacte, lactis, n. milk

lacus, -us, m. vat, lake, tank

laedo, -ere, laesi, laesus strike, harm

lana, -ae f. wool

languidus, -a, -um weak, feeble

lanternarius, -i, m. lamplighter, guide

lanx, lancis, f. dish

lapidarius, -a, -um of stone

lapis, lapidis, m. stone

lardum, -i, n. bacon

Lares, -ium, m. pl. the Lares (spirits that presided over and guarded a house from evil)

largiter (adv.) very much

larva, -ae, f. ghost, skeleton

lascivus, -a, -um playful, wanton

laticiavius, -a, -um distinguished

latruncularius, -i, m. petty thief, brignad

latus, -a, -um broad, wide, deep

latus, lateris, n. side

Laurens (Laurentis) of Laurentum (the area over which Lavinia's father, Latinus, ruled)

lautitia, -ae, f. elegance

lautus, -a, -um fine, neat

Lavinum, -i, n. the town founded by Aeneas after his voyage from Troy and marriage to the native princess Lavinia.

lavo, -ere, lavi, lautus wash, moisten

lecticarius, -i, m. liter-bearer

lectus, -i, m. couch, bed

legio, -ionis, f. legion (a division of the Roman army)

legitimus, -a, -um allowed by law, legal, proper, regular

lego (1) commission, appoint, bequeath

lego, -ere, lexi, lectus pick, gather, choose, read

lenio (4) appease, quiet

levis, -e light, slight

levo (1) lighten, raise

lex, legis, f. law

libella, -ae, f. a small silver coin (our "dime", actually ¼ denarius)

libellus, -i, m. small book, diary, small pamphlet, petition, placard, account-book

liber, libri, m. book

Liber, Liberi, m. Bacchus (god of wine)

liberalitas, -tatis, f. kindness, generosity

liberta, -ae, f. freedwoman

libertus, -i, m. freedman

libido, -dinis, f. desire, lust

libitinarius, -i, m. undertaker

libra, -ae, f. balance, pound (the origin of the sign of English Italian, and Turkish currency, which is a stylized L)

licet, licere, licuit (imper.) it is permitted

lictor, -oris, m. lictor

lignarus, -i, m. carpenter

ligo (1) tie, bind

limen, liminis, n. threshold, door

limensis, -e of Limenia (a town on N. African coast)

linteum, -i, n. linen, sail

liquamen, -minis, n. fish-sauce

littera, -ae, f. letter

litus, litoris, n. shore(line)

locatrix, -tricis, m. real-estate agent, contract

151

locus, -i, m. location, spot
place
lomentum, -i, n. bean meal
longe (adv.) far
longus, -a, -um long, lengthy
lucerna, -ae, f. lamp, light
Lucretianus, -a, -um Lucretius'
lucrum, -i, n. gain, profit
ludo, -ere, ludi, lusus play
ludus, -i, m. sport, game
lumen, luminis, n. light, lamp,
torch
luna, -ae, f. moon; when capitalized, Diana (goddess of the
moon)
luridus, -a, -um pale yellow,
dismal
luxa (1) dislocate
lympha, -ae, f. clear water

M

macellum, -i, n. produce-market
maculosus, -a, -um full of spots
madidus, -a, -um dripping, wet,
moist
magis (adv.) more
magister, magistri, m. master
magnitudo, -tudinis, f. size
magnus, -a, -um big, great
maiestas, -tatis, f. dignity,
treason
maior, maius (comp.) larger,
bigger
Maius, -a, -um of May (the 5th
month named after Maia, the
mother of Mercury)
maledico, -ere, -dixi, -dictus curse
malo, malle, malui prefer
malum, -i, n. evil, concern
malus, -i, m. apple; with *punicus,*
pomegranate
manceps, mancipis, m. pur-
chaser, contractor
mancipium, -i, n. property, slave
mandatus, -us, m. order, command
mane (adv.) in the morning;
with *bene,* early in the
morning

maneo, -ere, mansi, mansurus
remain
Manes, -ium, m. pl. the shades
(the deified souls of the dead
in the underworld); with *Dis,*
to the departed soul(s) of
manus, -us, f. hand, band
mappa, -ae, f. napkin
mare, maris, n. sea
margo, -ginis, c. edge, margin
Marianus, -a, -um Marius'
marinus, -a, -um of the sea
marmoratus, -a, -um of marble
marmoreus, -a, -um of marble
Mars, Martis, m. Mars (the god
of war)
Martius, -a, -um of March (the
month named after Mars)
mater, matris, f. mother
matella, -ae, f. pot
maxime (adv.) especially
maximus, -a, -um greatest,
largest
meatus, -us, m. going, motion
medicus, -i, m. physician,
doctor
medium, -i, n. middle
mehercule (interj.) by God!
mel, mellis, n. honey
melior, melius (comp.) better
mellusculus, -a, -um somewhat
better
mellitus, -a, -um of honey
memini (defect.) remember
mendacium, -i, n. lie, falsehood
mendosus, -a, -um full of defects,
faulty
mens, mentis, f. mind
mensa, -ae, f. table
mensis, -is, f. month
mensor, -oris, m. surveyor
mensura, -ae, f. measure(ment),
size
mentum, -i, n. chin
mercatus, -us, m. traffic, fair,
market
merces, mercidis, f. pay, wages
fee
Mercurius, -i, m. Mercury (god
of commerce & theft, messenger of the gods)

merens (-entis) deserving

mereo, -ere, merui, meritus serve

mergo, -ere, mersi, mersus sink, dip, immerse

meritorius, -i, m. decoration, ornament

meritum, -i, n. service, kindness

merum, -i, n. pure unmixed wine

mesopudium, -i, n. the sum of ½ as

metus, -us, m. fear, dread, terror

meus, -a, -um my

miles, militis, m. soldier

milia, -ium, n. pl. thousands

milito (1) campaign, fight

milium, -i, n. millet

mille (indecl.) a thousand

mil(l)iarium, -i, n. milestone

milvus, -i, m. bird of prey

minimus, -a, -um least, smallest

minister, -tri, m. servant, priest

minor, minus (comp.) less, smaller

Minotaurus, -i, m. the Minotaur (a monster produced by the union of Minos of Crete's queen and a bull, which was confined in the Labyrinth)

minus (adv.) less

minutatim (adv.) bit by bit, little by little

miraculum, -i, n. wonder, marvel

miror (1) wonder at

Misenensis, -e of Misenum (the town on top of the tip of the northern peninsula on the Bay of Naples)

Misenum, -i, N. Misenum

miser, misera, miserum sad, wretched

miseror (1) pity, bemoan

missio, -ionis, f. discharge, release, end

mitto, -ere, misi, missus send

mixi — perf. of misceo, have sexual intercourse with

mobilis, -e pliant, fickle

modius, -i, m. bushel, measure

modo (adv.) just, recently, only

mola, -ae, f. millstone, mill

molestus, -a, -um irksome, annoying; moleste fero, be greatly annoyed

mollis, -e, soft, mild, calm, tender

mons, montis, m. mount(ain)

monumentum, -i, n. memorial, monument

mora, ae, f. delay, postponement

morator, -oris, m. delayer, lounger

mores, -um, f. pl. habits, customs

morior, mori, mortuus die, be dead

moror (1) delay

mors, mortis, f. death

mortuus, -a, -um dead

mortuus, -i, m. dead man

mosimoris, m. custom, fashion, mood

motus, -us, m. motion, movement; with terrae, earthquake

moveo, -ere, movi, motus move

mox (adv.) next, soon

mulier, -ieris, f. woman

mulio, -ionis, m. mule-driver, mule-dealer

mulsum, -i, n. honey-wine, mead

multo (adv.) much

multum (adv.) much

multus, -a, -um many (a), much

mulus, -i, m. mule

mundus, -i, m. world, universe

munerarius, -i, m. exhibitor of gladiators

municeps, -cipis, m. inhabitant, citizen

munificentia, -ae, f. generosity

munimentum, -i, n. protection

munio (4) build, fortify

munus, muneris, n. show, gift, duty

muria, -ae, f. brine, pickle

murus, -i, m. wall
mus, muris, c. mouse
muto (1) change, alter

N

nactus, -a, -um — from *nanciscor*, find
nam (conj.) for
narratio, -ionis, f. narrative
nascor, nasci, natus be born, be protected
naufrago (1) be wrecked
nausea, -ae, f. vomit
navicula, -ae, f. small boat
navis, -is, f. ship
nepos, nepotis, m. grandson
nec (conj.) nor, and not
necesse (indecl.) necessary
nemo (irregular) no one
ne...quidem (adv.) not even...
neque (conj.) nor
nescio, -ire not know
niger, nigra, nigrum black, dark
nihilominus (adv.) nonetheless
nil — a common variant of *nihil*, nothing
nisi (conj.) unless, except
niteo, -ere, nitui shine, gleam
nix, nivis, f. snow
nobilis, -e well known, noble
Nola, -ae, f. Nola (a city NE of Pompeii, the birthplace of the Emperor Augustus)
nolo, nolle, nolui be unwilling; in its imperative *noli(te)* with an infinitive, don't...!
nomen, nominis, n. name
nomino (1) name, title
non (adv.) not
Nonae, -arum, f. pl. the Nones (the 7th day of all months but March, July, October, & May, when they are on the 5th day)
nondum (adv.) not yet
nongenti, -ae, -a nine hundred
nonus, -a, -um ninth
nos, nobis (per. pron.) we
nosco, -ere, novi, notus learn, know

noster, nostra, nostrum our
nota, -ae, f. mark, sign, note
noto (1) note, mark
novem (indecl.) nine
Novembris, -e of November (the 9th month in the old Roman calendar)
novus, -a, -um new, fresh, strange
nox, noctis, f. night
nubes, -is, f. cloud, mist
Nuceria, -ae, f. the town immediately to the west of Pompeii
Nuc(h)erini, -orum, m. pl. the people of Nuceria
nudus, -a, -um bare, naked
nullus, -a, -um no
numen, numinis, n. divine power, divinity, spirit
numero (1) number, count
numerus, -i, m. number
num(m)eratus, -a, -um in cash
nummularius, -i, m. money-changer
nummus, -i, m. sesterce, coin, cash
numquam (adv.) never
nunc (adv.) now
nundinae, -arum, f.pl. market-day
nuntius, -i, m. messenger, message
nuper (adv.) recently
nuto (1) nod, waive
nux, nucis, f. nut, berry
Nysa, -ae, f. an area in Asia Minor (the modern Turkey sacred to Liber

O

ob (prep. + acc.) on-account-of
obduco, -ere, -duxi, -ductus extend, cover
obiter (adv.) incidentally
obiurgo (1) blame, rebuke
obstruo, -ere, struxi, -structus block, shut off
obversor (1) attend, be near (+ dat.)

occasio, -ionis, f. occasion
oceanus, -i, m. ocean
ocellus, -i, m. (dear little) eye
October, -bris, -bre of October
(the 8th month in the old
Roman calendar)
oculus, -i, m. eye
odiosus, -a, -um hateful
odor, -oris, m. odor, smell
Odyesia, -ae, f. Homer's *Odyssey*
officina, -ae, f. (work)ship
officium, -i, n. duty, attention
oletum, -i, n. olive-orchard
oliva, -ae, f. olive
omnis, -e all, every, entire
onagrus, -i, m. wild ass
onero (1) load, burden
onus, oneris, n. load, burden
operio, - ire, operui, opertus
cover (over)
opimus, -a, -um rich, fat, fertile
oportet, -ere, oportuit (imper.)
it is necessary
oppidum, -i, n. town
opportunus, -a, -um fit, suitable
opstruo, -ere, -struxi, structus
build, block, hinder
optimus, -a, -um best, excellent
ora, -ae, f. border, edge, coast,
region
orchestra, -ae, f. orchestra (the
central part of a theatre or
odeon)
Orcus, -i, m. god of the underworld
ordo, -dinis, f. order, formation,
council
orior, oriri, ortus rise
ornamentum, -i, n. decoration,
ornament
oro (1) ask, support
os, ossis, n. bone
os, oris, n. mouth, lip, face
ostarius, -i, m. doorkeeper
otiosus, -a, -um idle, unem-
ployed, quiet
otiosus, -i, m. loafer, idler
otium, -i, n. leisure, ease

Ovidius, -i, m. Ovid (the justly
renowned Roman poet in the
reign of Augustus who was ex-
iled to Tomi in modern
Romania by the First Em-
peror)

P

paene (adv.) almost
Paestum, -i, n. Paestum (an old
Greek town in southern Italy
below the Sorrento peninsula
with extensive remains and
exquisite temples)
paganus, -i, m. peasant, fellow-
villager
pagina, -ae, f. page
pagus, -i, m. region, district,
canton
palestra, -ae, f. gymnasium,
wrestling-ground
palea, -ae, f. chaff, straw
pallium, -i, n. cloak, mantle
pampineus, -a, -um of vines
panis, -is, m. bread
papaver, -veris, n. poppy
par, paris, c. match, pair
Parca, -ae, f. goddess of Fate
parens, -entis, c. parent
paries, -ietis, m. wall
paro (1) prepare, get ready
paropsis, -sidis f. dish
pars, partis, f. part, section
direction
parum (adv.) too little
parvus, -a, -um little, small
pascuum, -i, n. pasture, pasture-
rights
passum, -i, n. raisin-wine
pater, patris, m. father; with
patriae, father of the fatherland (a title sometimes given
by the Senate to the Emperor)
patera, -ae, f. saucer
patientia, -ae, f. patience, calm
patior, pati, passus allow,
endure, suffer
patria, -ae, f. fatherland
patrimonium, -i, n. estate, in-
heritance

patritus, -a, -um father's, ancestral

patronus, -i, m. protector, guardian

paulum (adv.) a little, somewhat

pavimentum, -i, n. floor, pavement

pecco (1) sin

peculium, -i, n. small savings, cache

pecunia, -ae, f. money

pelvis, -is, f. basin

pendeo, -ere, pependi hang

pensum, -i, n. portion of wool

peperi — perf. of *pario,* give birth

pequinia, -ae, f. money

per (prep. acc.) thru, by-means-of; *per se,* spontaneously

perbonus, -a, -um very nice

percutio, -tere, cussi, -cussus strike, beat

pereo, -ire, -ivi, -iturus perish be lost, die

pergula, -ae, f. verandah, balcony

periculum, -i, n. danger, peril

perinde (adv.) in the same manner, just as; with *ac,* just as if

perlego, -ere, -legi, -lectus scan

perpetuus, -a, -um permanent, consistent; in perpetuum, forever

persequor, -sequi, -secutus hunt for

persevero (1) continue, persist

persolvo, -ere, -solvi, -solutus bestow, pay

persuavissime (adv.) very sweetly

perterreo, -ere, -terrui, -territus terrify

pervenio, -ere, -veni, -ventus arrive

pes, pedis, m. foot

Petecusani, -orum, m. pl. the people of Petecus

peto, -ere, -ivi, -itus ask, seek for

philosophus, -i, m. professor

Phoebe, -is, f. Diana (goddess of the hunt & moon), the moon

pica, -ae, f. magpie

picatus, -a, -um pitchy; with *vinum,* wine that has a pitchy taste

pictor, -oris, m. artist

pictura, -ae, f. painting

pictus, -a, -um — from *pingo,* paint, represent, adorn

pietas, -tatis, f. sense of devotion, dutiful conduct

pilicrepus, -i, m. ball-player

pingo, -ere, pinxi, pictus paint, depict, draw

pinus, us, f. pinetree

piper, piperis, n. pepper

pistor, -oris, m. miller, baker

pisum, -i, n. pea

pittacium, -i, n. tap

pius, -a, -um revered, dutiful

placet, -ere, placuit (imper.) it seems best

plaga, -ae, f. blow, strike

planus, -a, -um level, flat

plausus, -us, m. applause, approbation

plenus, -a, -um full, sated, pregnant

pleps — a variant for *plebs,* the common people

ploro (1) weep for

pluit, -ere, pluit (imper.) it rains

plumbus, -i, m. lead

plures, pluria several

plurimus, -a, -um very many, numerous, hearty

plus (adv.) more

plus, pluris, n. more

podium, -i, n. platform, height base

poena, -ae, f. parade, procession

Pompeiani, -orum, m. pl. the people of Pompeii (a city on the coast of Campania, overwhelmed by the eruption of Vesuvius in 79 A.D.)

Pompeianus, -a, -umm of Pompeii, Pompeian

Pompeii, -orum, m. pl. the city of Pompeii

pomum, -i, n. fruit

pondo (adv.) by weight; with numerals as indecl. noun, pound(s)

pondus, -deris, n. weight

pono, -ere, posui, positus put; place

ponticulus, -i, m. little bridge

pontifex, pontificis, m. priest; with *maximus,* supreme priest (the Roman Emperor's title as well as today's Popes')

popina, -ae, f. cook-shop

populus, -i, m. people

porrigo, -ere, -rexi, -rectus reach out, extend

porta, -ae, f. gate

porticus, -us, f. portico, colonnade

porto (1) carry

posco, -ere, poposci demand, ask for

possideo, -ere, -sedi, -sessus take possession of, own

possum, posse, potui be able

post (prep. + acc.) after

postea (adv.) afterwards

posteri, -orum, m. pl. future generations, posterity

postis, -is m. post

postquam (conj.) after

postulo (1) demand, ask for

potestas, -tatis, f. power

potissimus, -a, -um the best, most able

poto (1) drink

praebeo, -ere, -bui, -bitus furnish, provide

praecedo, -ere, -cessi, -cessurus go before, surpass, advance

praecellens (-entis) extraordinary

praecipue (adv.) chiefly

praedium, -i n. estate, farm

praefectus, -i, m. prefect

praefero, -ferre, -tuli, -latus display, prefer

praenuntius, -i, m. foreteller, omen

praepono, -ere, -posui, -positus put...in charge of (+ dat.)

praesto (adv.) at hand, present

praesum, -esse, -fui be in charge of (+ dat.)

praeter (prep. + acc.) except

praeterea (adv.) in addition

praetereo, -ire, -ivi, -iturus omit

praetextatus, -a, -um wearing the virile toga

praetor, -oris, m. chief-justice (the second highest spot on the political ladder known as the *cursus honorum*)

praevaleo, -ere, valui be stronger, prevail

prastinatus, -a, -um clad in leek-green

premo, -ere, -pressi, pressus press, crush

prendo, -ere, prendi, prensus grasp, seize, arrest

pretium, -i, n. price, reward, value

pridie (prep. + acc.) on-the-day-before

primus, -a, -um first

prioriprius (comp. adj.) earlier

privatus, -i, -um private, individual

privatus, -i, m. private owner

pro (pre. + abl.) for, on-behalf-of, in-place-of)

probitas, -tatis, f. uprightness, honesty

probo (1) approve, recommend, prove

probus, -a, -um excellent, proper, up-right, honorable

procedo, -ere, cessi, -cessurus go forth, advance

proconsule (indecl.) proconsul (a man who has served in all the Roman offices of state)

procurator, -oris, m. baliff, manager

procuro (1) have charge of, attend to, administer

produco, -ere, -duxi, -ductus lead forth, draw up

profectus, -a, -um – from *proficiscor,* set out

progredior, -gredi, -gressus go (forth), proceed

proicio, -cere, -ieci, -iectus throw throw forth

promulsidare, -aris n. tray

pronepos, -potis, m. great-grandson

prope (prep. + acc.) near

propero (1) haste, be in a hurry

propinquus, -a, -um near(by)

propitius, -a, -um favorable

proprius (adv.) nearer

propter (prep. + acc.) on-account-of, due to

proripio, -ere, -ripui, -reptus hurry forth, rush out

prout (conj.) just as, according to, now

proximus, -a, -um nearest, most recent; *ex proximo,* from close at hand

prunum, -i, n. plum

publice (adv.) at public expense

publicus, -a, -um common, public

pudor, -oris, m. shame, sense of honor, modesty

puella, -ae, f. girl

puer, pueri, m. boy

pugna, -ae, f. fight

pugno (1) fight

pumex, pumicis, m. pumice-stone

Punicus, -a, -um of Carthage

pupa, -ae, f. girl, damsel, "doll"

purgamentum, -i, n. dirt, filth

purgo (1) clean, sort

pusillum (adv.) very little

pusillus, -a, -um very little, paltry

Puteolani, -orum, m. pl. the people of Puteoli (chief port of Rome on the coast of Campania until the lst century A.D., the modern Pozzuoli with the old forum yet visible)

puto (1) think

pyxis, -idis f. small box

Q

qua (conj.) where

quadratarius, -i, m. stone-cutter

quadratus, -a, -um square

quadriremis, -is, f. quadrireme (a ship with 4 banks of oars)

quaero, -ere, quaesivi, quaesitus seek, ask

quaestor, -oris, m. treasurer (the 3rd highest position on the political ladder)

qualis, -e such, as

quam (part. after comp.) than

quamquam (conj.) although

quando (conj.) when

quare (conj.) why, therefore

quartum (adv.) for the fourth time

quartus, -a, -um fourth

quasi as if, as it were

quasso (1) shake, scatter

quatuor (indecl.) four

que (enclitic) and (attached to the word before which it is to be translated)

quemadmodum (conj.) just as, how

qui, quae, quod who, which, that

quia (conj.) because

quicumque, quaecumque, quod-cumque whoever, whatever

quidem (adv.) indeed

quiesco, -ere, quievi, quetus rest

quietes, -ei, f. rest, sleep

quingenti, -ae, -a five hundred

quinquaginta (indecl.) fifty

quinque (indecl.) five

quinquennalis, -is, m. special mayor (with a five year term)

quis, quid (inter. pron.) who? what?

quisquam, quaequam, quicquam anyone, anything

quisquis, quidquid (indef. pron.) whoever, whatever

quivis, quaevis, quodvis whoever, whatever

quneus, -i, m. wedge, theatre-seats

quod (conj.) because

quoque (adv.) also

R

ramus, -i, m. branch, bough
rapio, -pere, rapui, raptus carry off
raptim (adv.) hurriedly
rarus, -a, -um scattered, infrequent
ratio, -ionis, f. account
ratiocinor (1) compute, count
ratus, -a, -um — from *reor,* think
recens (recentis) fresh, new,
recipio, -ere, -cepi, -ceptus receive
recito (1) read out
recognosco, -ere, -novi, -bitus make known, learn
rectus, -a, -um straight, correct
recubo (1) lie back, recline
recuso (1) refuse
reddo, -ere, reddidi, redditus return, give back
redemo, -ere, -emi, -emptus buy back
redeo, -ire, -ii, -itus return, go back
redigo, -ere, -egi, -actus bring back, reduce, render, return
refero, -ferre, -tuli, -latus repeat, bring back
reficio, -ere, -feci, -fectus repair, make again
regina, -ae, f. queen
regio, -ionis, f. area
regno (1) rule, reign
regredior, -gredi, -gressus go back
reliquum, -i, n. remainder, revenue
reliquus, -a, -um remaining
reluceo, -ere, luxi shine, glow
remaneo, -ere, -mansi, -mansurus remain
repello, -ere, reppuli, repulsus drive back
reperio, -ire, reperi, repertus find, discover, learn
requesco, -ere, -quievi, -quietus rest
requiro, -ere, -quisivi, -quistus look for, miss

res, rei, f. thing, item, object
resido, -ere, -sedi sit down settle down
respicio, -ere, -spexi, -spectus look back
respondeo, -ere, spondi, -sponsus answer, reply
respublica, reipublicae, f. state, city
resupinatus, -a, -um on one's back
restituo, -ere, -stitui, -stitutus give back, restore, replace
retiarius, -i, m. net-fighter
retro (adv.) back(wards)
rettuli — perf. of *refero,* bring back
rex, regis, m. ruler, king
Rhodius, -a, -um of Rhodes (the largest of the group of Aegean Isles known as the Duodecanese at the SW corner of modern Turkey)
rideo, -ere, risi, risus smile at
rivalis, -is, m. neighbor, rival
rixo (1) brawl, quarrel
rogatus, -us, m. asking, request
rogo (1) ask, beg
Roma, -ae, f. Rome, the Eternal City (7 miles up the Tiber from the Sea)
ruber, rubra, rubrum reddish
ruina, -ae, f. fall, ruin, destruction
rumpo, -ere, rupi, reptus break, destroy
rursus (adv.) again, back
rusticus, -a, -um rural, country
rusticus, -i, m. peasant, "hick"
ruta, -ae, f. bitter herb

S

sacculus, -i, m. little bag
sacellus, -i, n. chapel
sacer, sacra, sacrum sacred, holy
sacerdos, -dotis, c. priest(ess)
sacra, -orum, m. pl. sacred rites
saepe (adv.) often
saltatio, -ianis, f. dance
salus, salutis, f. health, safety

saluto (1) greet

salve (interj.) hello! greetings!

salvus, -a, -um hallowed, holy

sarcina, -ae, f. baggage, pack

Sarnus, -i, m. the Sarnus River (a river in Campania, now 2 miles south of Pompeii but once by its gates, the modern Sarno)

satis (adv.) enough

satur, satum, saturum full of

Saturnalia, -ium, m. pl. the Saturnalia (the end-of-the-year festival to Saturn comparable to our Christmas)

Saturnus, -i, m. the father of the gods

Satyrus, -i, m. satyr (a sylvan creature associated with Pan)

saxum, -i, n. rock

scaena, -ae, f. stage

scaenicus, -i, m. actor, player

scala, -ae, f. step, ladder

scilicet (adv.) doubtless, of course

scio (4) know, realize

scolum, -i, m. seat

scomber, scombri, m. mackrel, tunafish

scopae, -arum, f. pl. twigs

scribo, -ere, scripsi, scriptus write

scriptor, -oris, m. writer, author

sculpo, -ere, sculpsi, sculptus carve

se, sibi (reflex. pron.) himself, herself, itself, themselves

secundum (prep. + acc.) next to

secundus, -a, -um following, favorable

securitas, -tatis, f. lack of concern, security

sed (conj.) but

sedeo, -ere, sedi, sessus sit, rest

sedes, -is, f. seat, chair, home

sella, -ae, f. seat, chair

semel (adv.) once; semel atque iterum, again and again

semen, seminis n. seed

semuncia, -ae. f. a half-ounce, trifle

seni, -ae, -a six (each)

sententia, -ae, f. sentence, feeling, decree

seplasium, -i, n. perfume

septem (indecl.) seven

septimus, -a, -um seventh

septingenti, -ae, -a seven hundred

septuaginta (indecl.) seventy

sepulchris, -e of a tomb, tomb-like

sepulchrum, -i, n. tomb

sepultura, -ae, f. burial, interment

sequor, sequi, secutus follow

seribibus, -i, m. late-drinker, drunk, sot

servo (1) preserve, save

servus, -i, m. slave, servant

sescenti, -ae, -a six hundred

sessorium, -i, n. residence

sestertius, -i, m. sesterce (a silver coin, the ordinary Roman unit in accounting, usually reckoned as worth 5 ¢ and abbreviated as HS)

Setinus, -a, -um of Setia (a town in Latium, the modern Sezze, renowned for its wine)

seviratus, -us, m. commission-ership

sex (indecl.) six

sextilis, -e of sextilis (the former name for the month of August)

sextus, -a, -um sixth

si (conj.) if

sic (adv.) thus, so

siccus, -a, -um dry

signaculum, -i, n. mark, sign, signet-ring

signator, -oris, m. painter

signatorius, -a, -um sealing

signo (1) seal, secure, record

signum, -i, n. mark, seal, statue

similis, -e like, similar to (+ dat.)

sine (prep. + abl.) without

singulus, -a, -um separate, single, each

sinister, -stra, -strum left

siqui (conj.) if indeed

sitiens (-ientis) thirsty, dry, parched

sitio, -ere thirst, be dry

Sittianus, -a, -um Sittius'

sive (con.) or if; sive...sive, whether...or

sodalis, -is, c. companion, friend

sol, solis, m. sun; when capitalized, Apollo (the god of the sun)

solea, -ae, f. sandal, shoe

soleo, -ere, solitus (semidep.) be accustomed (+ inf.)

solum, -i, n. site, soil

solus, -a, -um only, alone

somnus, -i, m. sleep

sonantior, sonantius (comp.) rather noisy

sordidus, -a, -um dirty, squalid

spargo, -ere, sparsi, sparsus scatter, sprinkle

sparsio, -ionis, f. sprinkling

spatium, -i, n. space, distance

species, -ei, f. appearance, sight

spectaculum, -i, n. exhibition, public show

spes, spei, f. hope

spiritus, -us, m. breath(ing) air

spolium, -i, n. spoils, plunder

Stabiae, -arum, f. pl. Stabiae (a small resort town across the bay from Naples, buried by the eruption of Vesuvius, the modern Castellamare)

Stabianus, -a, -um of Stabiae

stabulum, -i, n. inn

statera, -ae, f. balance

statim (adv.) immediately, at once

statua, -ae, f. image, statue

stella, -ae, f. star

stercorarius, -i, m. befouler, defiler

'stercus, -i, m. manure

sternuto (1) sneeze, snore

stipendium, -i, n. campaign, season

stipulatus, -us, m. bargain, agreement

sto, -are, steti, staturus stand

strepitus, -us, m. dim, clatter

structor, -oris, m. mason, carpenter

studium, -i, n. eagerness, pursuit, study

stultus, -a, -um dull, stupid

stupeo, -ere, -ui be amazed at

suavis, -e sweet, pleasant

sub (prep. + abl.) under, at the foot of

subiaceo, -ere, -iacui be situated near (+ dat.)

subinde (adv.) just after

subito (adv.) suddenly

sublatus, -a, -um — from *tollo*, remove

subscribo, -ere, -scripsi, -scriptus write below

suburbanus, -a, -um suburban

succingo, -ere, -cinxi, -cinctus gird

sulphur, -uris, n. sulphur (the yellow, powdery, and distinctive chemical whose sign is S)

summus, -a, -um top of, highest; *ad summum,* finally

super (prep. + acc.) above, over, on

superi, -orum, m. pl. the gods

superstes (-stitis) surviving

supersum, -esse, fui survive (+ dat.)

supplex, -plicis, c. suppliant

supplico (1) pray for

suppositicius, -i, m. substitute

supra (adv.) above

surgo, -ere, surrexi, surrectus rise, get up

Surrentiunus, -a, -um of Surrentum (a town on the famous penninsula in southern Campania, the modern Sorrento)

suscipio, -ere, -cepi, -ceptus support, undertake, enter into

suspendo, -ere, -pendi, -pensus hang (up), prop up, depend

suspensus, -a, -um doubtful, anxious

suspirium, -i, n. deep breath, sigh

sustineo, -ere, -tenui, -tentus
support

sustuli — from *tollo,* raise, convey, remove

susum (adv.) upper, above

suus, -a, -um his, her, its, their own

Syriacus, -a, -um of Syria

T

tabella, -ae, f. writing-tablet, voting tablet

taberna, -ae, f. stall, tavern, inn; shop, lodging

tabesco, -ere, -ui fade, pine away

tabula, -ae, f. table, account-book; with *opus,* treasury building

taedium, -i, n. weariness, nonsense, irksomeness

talis, -e such (a)

tam (adv.) so, thus, as

tamen (adv.) nevertheless, yet, still

tamquam (adv.) as if

tandem (adv.) at last, finally

tango, -ere, tetigi, tactus touch

tantus, -a, -um so great

tarde (adv.) later

Tascum, -i, n. Tascum (a small town near Misenum on the N side of the Bay of Naples)

Tauromenitanus, -a, -um of Taormina (a resort town on the E side of Sicily near Mt. Etna)

tectum, -i, n. dwelling, house

tego, -ere, texi, tectus cover

tegula, -ae, f. tile

Telesinus, -a, -um of Telesia (a town of Samnium, the modern village of Telese)

templum, -i, n. sacred area, temple

tempto (1) attempt

tempus, temporis, n. time

teneo, -ere, tenui, tentus hold, keep

tengomenae, -arum, f. pl. whistle-wetting act

tergum, -i, n. back

terra, -ae, f. earth, land

terrera, -ae, f. square, die, token, ticket

territorium, -i, n. land round a town, domain

terror, -oris, m. dread, horror, fear

tertium (adv.) for the third time

tertius, -a, -um third

testamentum, -i, n. will, testament

textor, -oris, m. weaver

theatrum, -i, m. theatre (a place for seeing various types of shows)

therma, -ae, f. a public bath; as pl., a thermal establishment

thyminus, -a, -um made of thyme

timeo, -ere, timui be afraid of, fear

timor, oris, m. fear, dread, alarm

Tironianus, -a, -um Tiron's

titulus, -i, m. inscription, ticket placard, title

tomaculum, -i, n. sausage

tonsor, -oris, m. barber

torqueo, -ere, torsi, tortus twist

torus, -i, m. knot, couch

tot (indecl.) so many

totus, -a, -um all, entire

transeo, -ire, -ivi, -iturus pass by

trecenties (adv.) 300 times

tremor, -oris, m. trembling, tremor

trepidans (-antis) trembling, fearful

trepidatio, -ionis, f. agitation, hurry

tres, tria three

triangularis, -e triangular

tribunal, -alis, n. raised platform, judgement seat, cenotaph

tribunicius, -a, -um tribunician, belonging to a tribune (a political office reserved for the common people and the soldiers)

tribunus, -i, m. tribune

triclinium, -i, dining-room

Trifolinus, -a, -um of Mt. Trifolium (near Naples and renowned for its grapes)

triginta (indecl.) thirty

tristis, -e sad, severe

triticum, -i n. wheat

Troia, -ae, f. Troy (a city on the Dardanelles in the NW corner of modern Turkey, sacked by the Greeks in a trade war in the 12th century B.C. and now excavated)

Troianus, -i, m. Trojan, an inhabitant of Troy

truncus, -i, m. tree trunk

tu, tui, tibi, te (pers. pron.) you

tum (adv.) then

tumultor (1) make a disturbance

tumultus, -us, m. noise, confusion

tunc (adv.) then, at that time

tunica, -ae, f. tunic (the ordinary sleeved garment worn by both sexes)

turba, -ae, f. disorder, row, mob

turpis, -e, base, disgusting

tutor, -oris, m. defender, guard

tuus, -a, -um your

U

udus, -a, -um wet, damp

umquam (adv.) ever

una (adv.) together

uncus, -i, hook, barb

unda, -ae, f. wave, water

unde (adv.) whence

ungentarius, -i, m. perfume-dealer

unguentum, -i, n. perfume

universus, -a, -um whole, entire, altogether

unus, -a, -um one

urbs, urbis, f. city

urna, -ae, f. pot, jar, urn

uro, -ere, ussi, ustus burn, scorch, sting

ursa, -ae, f. mother-bear

ursus, -i, m. bear

usura, -ae, f. interest

usus, -us, m. use, employment

ut (conj. + indic.) when, as

ut (conj. + subj.) so that

uter, utris, m. bag

uterque, utraque, utrumque each

utinam (part. with subj.) would that!

utor, uti, usus use, employ (+ abl.)

uva, -ae, f. grapes, vine

uxor, -oris, f. wife, spouse

V

valde (adv.) of course, very

valdus, -a, -um strong, mighty

valvae, -arum, f. pl. folding-doors

vagitus, -us, m. crying, waiting

vagor (1) wander, roam

varius, -a, -um striped, multicolored

vas, vasis, dish, vessel, baggage

vasculum, -i, n. small vessel or dish

vastus, -a, -um empty, vast, immense

vectigal, -alis, n. tax, toll, rent

vel (part.) or

velo (1) cover

vello, -ere, velli, vulsus pluck, pull

velum, -i, n. sail, awning

venatio, -ionis, f. hunting spectacle, chase

vendo, -ere, vendi, venitus sell

venerius, -a, -um lovely, of Venus

venio, -ire, veni, venturus come

ventus, -i, m. wind

Venus, Veneris, f. Venus (goddess of love); love affair

verbum, -i, n. word, phrase

verecundus, -a, -um shy, reserved, modest

vernaculus, -a, -um native

vero (adv.) indeed

vertebra, -ae, f. joint

verto, -ere, -verti, versus turn, change

versus, -a, -um true, real, just

vestarius, -i, m. tailor, clothes-dealer

vestigium, -i, n. track, spot
vestimentum, -i n. clothing
vestis, -is, f. cloth
Vesubius, -i, m. Vesuvius (the famous volcanic mountain overlooking the bay of Naples)
Vesuvianus, -a, -um of Vesuvius
veteranus, -i, m. veteran, experienced soldier
veto, -are, ui, -tus forbid, prohibit
vetus (verteris) old, pristine, ancient
via, -ae, f. road, street
viator, -oris, m. traveller
vibro (1) shake, hurl
viceni, -ae, -a twenty (each)
vicinia, -ae, f. neighborhood
vicinus, -i, m. neighbor
victor (-oris) victorious
victoria, -ae, f. victory
vicus, -i, m. village
video, -ere, vidi, visus see
videor, videri, visus seem
vigil, vigilis, m. fireman
vigilo (1) watch, keep awake, be watchful
viginti (indecl.) twenty

vilicus, -i, m. baliff
villa, -ae, f. countryhouse, villa
vincio, -ire, vinci, vinctus tie, bind
vinco, -ere, vici, victus win, overcome
vinea, -ae, f. vineyard
vinum, -i, n. wine
violo (1) outrage, violate
violentia, -ae, f. vehemence, ferocity
vipera, -ae, f. snake
vir, viri, m. man, husband
viridis, -e green, pleasant
virta, -ae, f. an unidentified herb
vis, vis f. force, violence
visus, -us, m. vision, sight, appearance
vita, -ae, f. life
vitreus, -a, -um of glass
vivo, -ere, vixi, victurus live, be alive
vivus, -a, -um alive
vix (adv.) scarcely, hardly
vaco (1) call
volo, velle, volui wish, be willing
volo (1) fly
voltus, -us, m. look, appearance
vos, vobis (per. pron.) y'all
vox, vocis, f. voice